Wake-Up Call in the Wee Hours

Wake-Up Call in the Wee Hours

"Arise awake and stop not till your goal is achieved."

– *Swami Vivekananda*

Vinay Kr Mittal

and

Ambika Mittal

A Sterling Paperback

STERLING PAPERBACKS
An imprint of
Sterling Publishers (P) Ltd.
A-59, Okhla Industrial Area, Phase-II,
New Delhi-110020.
Tel: 26387070, 26386209; Fax: 91-11-26383788
E-mail: sterlingpublishers@airtelbroadband.in
ghai@nde.vsnl.net.in
www.sterlingpublishers.com

Wake-Up Call in the Wee Hours
© 2006, Vinay Kr Mittal and Ambika Mittal
ISBN 81 207 3075 6

All rights are reserved.
No part of this publication may be reproduced, stored in a retrieval system or transmitted, in any form or by any means, mechanical, photocopying, recording or otherwise, without prior written permission of the original publisher.

Published by Sterling Publishers Pvt. Ltd., New Delhi-110 020.
Printed at Sterling Publishers Pvt. Ltd., New Delhi-110020.

Dedication

"Greatest challenge lies for those, who set their first foot on the paths to destinations unexplored!"

This book is dedicated first and foremost to our parents, who gave us the opportunity to explore this life and this beautiful world.

It is dedicated to our all those teachers and professors, who enabled us to reach heights in this journey of knowledge.

This book is also dedicated to those torch-bearers and mentors of all ages and places, who have laid or continue to lay down their lives towards enabling and helping others to set their first foot on journeys to various destinations all around.

We further dedicate this book to all dreamers and achievers of all times and places, whose vision and performance have always laid first foundation stone, towards creating and providing an environment for people alive by heart or mind or by both.

Authors

Foreword

This book is neither readymade-solution oriented, nor it is going to suggest you any quick-fix approaches or formulae. Unlike other self-help books available around, the aim of this book is mainly to trigger some questions – important for your life, and set some thinking process in you.

We believe that solutions to your problems lie in you only. You are very much capable of and are endowed with – powers and potentials to overcome any challenge or hurdle you ever come across, in your journey of life. However many of us, do not even have the realisation of our current state or of direction where we are heading to, and therefore feel miserable at times.

It requires an awakening in us, at first level. Next, we need to be mentally ready to accept the realities and hardships of life. Further to overcome adversities and challenges, one needs internal-external triggers, some catalysts and conducive environment. That is the role we would like ourselves to be confined to, through this book for you.

This book is mainly the medium for us to reach to you, and explore further possibilities.

Authors

Acknowledgement

Every creation has always contributions in its back-drop from people and sources, which are noticed sometimes or which go unsung at times.

A word of 'thanks' to all those who have either been a cause or an instrument of, or who have contributed towards a mission-seems very small.

However, we take this opportunity to express our heartfelt thanks to all those special people, and acknowledge their direct or indirect contributions to this first step towards our mission.

While mentioning all those special people, we wish to include especially:-

- Our parents, our children and all other family members, close friends, well-wishers and relatives – for imbibing us with right state of mind, environment and encouragement.
- All teachers, preachers, mentors and saints – for enabling us and equipping us constantly towards this journey.
- All professionals involved in publishing, printing and distribution of this book – for their dedicated, tireless and constant efforts for achieving excellence in this journey.
- Our friend 'Arun Thaplial' who gave shape to our ideas in the form of illustrations.
- All those dreamers, achievers and visionaries, who have laid the path before all to believe, that – *you can!*

Authors

Contents

Dedication	v
Foreword	vii
Acknowledgement	viii
Introduction	1

PART – I
THUNDERBOLT: A JOLT OF LIFE!

1.	A Whisper in Silence	7
2.	A Story Untold: The Journey of Life	17

Preparatory Stage-Transitions in Past: From Where to Where You have Travelled?

Middle Stage-Transitions in Present: How Things Change You?

Final Stage-Your Future: A Possibility-If You Don't Wake-Up Now!

PART – II
WHAT WENT WRONG?

3.	Is There Any Fault in System Programming?	45
4.	What is Malfunction in the System?	52
5.	Myths Created	58
6.	Misplaced Priorities and Wrong Programming	64
7.	The Wee-Hours!	71

PART – III
UNDERSTAND THE PROCESS!

8.	Three Types of People	79
9.	The 5 S's and Human Needs	86
10.	Five Healths and a Balanced Life	95
11.	Four Ways of Making Money and Education	107
12.	Four Levels of Work	120
13.	The Hidden Secrets	127

PART – IV
THE WAY OUT!

14.	Wake-Up Calls	139
15.	Are You Worried – Find Your Dream and Be a Player	145
16.	Think and Analyse	154
17.	Solution Steps: What Should You Do? What Can You Do? How Can You Succeed?	163

Introduction

People in the world who are creative and who believe in creative abilities can be divided into two categories.

The first category is of people alive by heart. They either possess some artistic talents or they support, like, put efforts-in and eventually excel in the domains of right-half side faculties of the brain.

These are the people who have been making this world more beautiful and pleasant to live in all times and places across the globe. Arts, crafts, music, dance, literature, drama, theatre, movie, poetry, songs etc., – all areas of an endless list, which give us uplifting emotions and touch the cords of our heart-are the fields of interest and creation of these people.

The second category is of people alive by mind. They have creative inclinations, interests and abilities. They are naturally inclined to, believe-in, put-in efforts and eventually succeed in the domains of left-half side faculties of the brain.

These are the people who have been making this world more comfortable, convenient and in-turn more enjoying to live-in all ages, environment and circumstances.

These are also the people, who in their quest to conquer know no limitations and no boundaries. Their journey of self-quest benefits human species of all geographies and of all generations.

Numerous inventions, discoveries and on-going research and development in all walks of life, be it medicine, science, engineering, technology, para-sciences, philosophy etc. – which all are the creation of mind-are the subjects of interest and areas of work of these people.

Most of the times, all dreamers and achievers also belong to either of these above two categories.

Now here is a 'question for you':-

"Which category of people do 'you belong to'?"

Or in case, you do not belong to either of the following categories as on now, then-

"Which category of people 'you want to become'?"

(a) Alive by heart
(b) Alive by mind
(c) Alive by heart and mind both
(d) A dreamer or an achiever – You have a dream or you have ever dreamt of achieving something in life.
(e) None of the above – You are or you want to continue to be a mere audience in an auditorium to clap or be a mere passenger in a vehicle (like a train) lead by drivers. Or you spend your life either as a parasite or as a mere earthworm – the crawling, crying, helpless, poor creature – or as some unnecessary load on mother earth–and still you do not want to change yourself or your life.

A Challenge: An Advice

If your answer to the above question is not '(a), (b), (c) or (d)' then do not read this book any further for it is neither written for you, nor you are fit to take benefit from this book.

But, if you do belong to either of the first four categories of people mentioned as above, (i.e. your answer to the above question is (a), (b), (c) or (d)), or if you have ever wished, thought, dreamt of being one of those, or you still aspire to be one of those, or if you either have ever dreamt of achieving anything in your life, or you have any dream to pursue, then- you may like to carry on reading this book further.

You may expect an adventurous, thrilling, exciting, enjoying and a mind-boggling journey ahead.

Our heartiest congratulations and salutations to you!

As you are the person we are searching for, and also because, this book is written for the benefit of people like you only – who are or who believe-in, or who have a dream of being one or have ever dreamt of being one of those movers and shakers of the world.

The kind of people, who live-by or who are at least alive by either their heart or by mind or by both, and who are the real performers and achievers.

This book is intended to reach, help and benefit also those people-who are or who have ever been disgusted, victimised or mocked upon by the parasites, incompetent and the odd forces of the world.

This book is also written for those-who want to contribute some beauty, comfort, pleasure to this world and to the human-kind, through their flair and talent in either of arts, crafts or sciences.

This book will help you to understand, feel and realise – how you can contribute more effectively to this world? How you can champion your cause and pursue your dreams? How can you achieve your goals by tuning minds, joining hands and working with people of similar thoughts, interests and beliefs, in order to overcome all obstacles? And, how can you do so, while claiming your rightfully first right to be yourself a beneficiary too? This is a part of our mission.

You are welcome in the journey together further!

Part – I

Thunderbolt: A Jolt of Life!

1

A Whisper in Silence

"Where are you going?" – somebody had whispered in my ears while I was in deep sleep or in a long, self-imposed trance probably. I remember my sleep was not that comfortable because of disturbances, so it must have been self-imposed trance only. I just woke up and sat down on my bed. My wife and children were still fast asleep. It was past midnight. I looked at the watch. The time was 3 am. I decided to take a stroll in my balcony. It was still night around-dark and silent, with dark clouds in the *sky*! Only the sole-traveller at night, moon was showing its cool bright light off and on.

I recollected then a short story once told by a wise man (a saint), and its characters just appeared to be alive in front of my eyes.

A short story (As told by a wise man)

There was an old man, living with his only daughter, in a hut by a riverside in a hill-town. He used to collect herbs from jungle and sell it to tourists at a nearby tourist spot, for his livelihood. Getting-up early every morning, collecting herbs in the jungle till noon, selling them till afternoon and then returning back home before sunset, was his daily routine. On returning home, the old man used to relax on a cot outside his hut, till his daughter would call him and serve him dinner. Then he would go asleep, to begin a similar routine next day too.

His daughter was of marriageable age. A young girl though had little schooling but was a wise girl. Many times she used to think and ask her father questions like "Why God created us? What for is this life? What should I do in my life? Why can't we improve our life? Father, why don't you do some study daily and do social work? Why should not you live a life of some significance and achieve some higher goals in life?"

But the old man would merely give some routine answers to make her quiet by saying things like, "Oh! My sweet

Father! Day is over it's fallen dark....! ....put the lamp ON?

daughter, why do you trouble yourself with such stupid questions? Why do you worry? I am still having long way to live. We should now enjoy food. Then I would tell you stories of my experiences today. We still have enough life remaining. Do not worry, enjoy life." And their life continued like that.

One evening, the old man returned early and he was relaxing on the cot in their courtyard as usual, when his daughter came out. She asked him, "Father, the day is over and it has fallen dark now. Should we lighten us up by putting the lamp on?"

The old man heard it, and was just lost in deep thoughts. Words started ringing in his mind. Next morning, instead of going to the jungle he went to people of his community. And with their help he fixed-up marriage of his daughter with a school teacher. With full fanfare he bade goodbye to his lovely daughter after her marriage next day.

A Whisper in Silence ■ 9

Following morning, when the sun was still orange the old man started his journey to be a monk. These words were still ringing in his mind, like thunderbolts – "Day is over... lighten us up... put the lamp on!" Well, the old man had set course to lighten himself up, before his life was over.

Ringing of words
Words, whispered in my ears, were still ringing in *my mind* loud and clear:-
WHERE are you going?
  Where are **YOU** *going?*
GOING
    Where are you

    WH...ERE are Y...OU GO...I...NG??

God · Status · Money
Helping others · Fun · Country
Charity · Society · Family · Name

My paces increased in the balcony. I was restless now. Somebody had just opened a pandora-box of numerous experiences and of strange questions imprinted deep in my mind, but unanswered yet.

Where you wanted to go?

Scenes of some classroom discussions of my past came alive, when I was discussing with my classmates Ajay, Yogesh, Shekhar, Arvind, Devesh and all, while we all were still in our 12th class of schooling. We were discussing about our future, which was then imminent shortly after a few months:-

... Ajay was convinced with the notion that money is everything, therefore he wanted to join his father's business and spend money on an extravagant lifestyle. Yogesh came from a middle-class family. He said, "I think, I will go on to do graduation in science, pick-up a job and help my parents economically. What do you think Arun? Will it be too difficult for me?" The question was addressed to me. I looked for a while at the expectant eyes of under-confident Yogesh and said, " Not at all difficult for you Yogesh. I am sure you can do even better!"....

.... While saying so, previous night's pictures had been reeling in front of me, when Arvind and myself were on a post-dinner walk and we had shared some of our intense inner-thoughts. I remember, Arvind had a dream to be a doctor, serve masses of rural India, and serve people who cannot afford doctor's fee or cannot even buy medicines.

A picture had appeared then in my mind of a poor village. A village – 'of people having barely any clothes to cover their bodies, pale faces and weak cattle due to one time meals only, children playing and fighting in dust instead of learning something in school, no electricity, and men-folk drinking liquor to spoil their already weak bodies further'...

.... And I had dreamt then that, 'If Arvind gives them medical-care, I help to provide them enough work and full-time meals, and with the help of friends and other groups

we teach them ill-effects of liquor', then we could imagine a different prosperous village.

.... A village – 'where kids go to school in neat dresses, and ladies sing even while doing all their house-core jobs like-feeding cattle, cleaning courtyards or carrying lunch for their beloved husbands! A village, where men-folk exercise

in village gymnasium or *akharas* (wrestling schools), and plough fields with healthy bulls or modern tractors'...

At that moment, Shekhar had interrupted the reeling pictures in my mind. Shekhar had said, "My dream is to be an engineer, go to States and do some research work there.

Here is hardly any scope of research in India. Don't you think so Devesh?" To which, Devesh had replied, "My mother would not allow me to go abroad. I would probably try to be a professor of mathematics here only. What about you Arun?"...

And, I had been thinking then, that – 'would there be any time, when people from abroad would be aspiring to come to India for doing research? How and when would it happen? Can I do something about it and what?'... ...

And I was then asking myself the question, "Where you wanted to go, Arun?"

Where are you going?

I noticed that, my paces in my balcony had stopped. I was thinking that, yesterday only I had heard these words again- "What about you Arun?" ...Where was it? Who had said it? Yes! I remember now. I had gone to Kapoors' marriage anniversary party yesterday night with my wife, the scenes of which started floating in front of me then.

There I had heard Mr Rao boasting of how he had won his boss, just by little buttering and by speaking his bosses' language. His success theory was, "Do whatever your boss wants. Even, if he says – polish my shoes, you do it, I will do it, because then he will not question me for-how much commission I took from the contractor."

Mrs Shah was displaying her new necklace and was commenting on her pot-bellied husband, "See friends, how beautiful this diamond-necklace is, which my hubby gifted me on my birthday yesterday. How cleverly he fooled income-tax officials at raid yesterday. I had thought him to be pig-headed all these years, but sometimes this boy does OK jobs."

Mr Dutt was commenting to few glittering ladies, "I don't know how come Mrs Arun still retains her charms in simple clothes, without wearing much jewellry even?" I figured, Mr Dutt belonged to that intellectual class of people, who believed in eat, drink and be merry culture. He was a professor of physics and by taking private tuitions itself he had made his fortune. All his college-days ideals had shattered and instead of spreading knowledge, he was selling his knowledge mercilessly now. But, sometimes Mr Dutt would share his heart to me, "Arun, people think I am successful. All these folks do get impressed by my big car and my big bungalow. Even District Collector and IG Police send their children to me for tuition. I have social status. But all this is not what I wanted to be. Nothing can be done now. My life has gone waste. So, I try to forget my pain in this glass of Whiskey."

Yes, at this Mrs Joshi had asked me something. Mrs Joshi was a learned lady. Her husband, a police inspector was known for his nefarious connections with the underworld and he had made his fast bucks through them. But Mrs Joshi, in the name of social service, used to woo public sympathy and media glares by donating to orphanages and destitute homes occasionally. As far as I knew, her heart was still alive but dust of money's lust had overpowered her goodness. Still she talked sense sometimes.

She must have seen me sitting there silent, while I was sipping lemonade. I was overhearing that time a discourse by Mr Singh, being given to mute audience of his glorious past, when he was young, rich and flamboyant. In fact, that moment, I was analysing the life of all those self-indulged,

so-called successful people. That was the time when Mrs Joshi had asked me aloud, "What about you Mr Arun? Why are you not coming out with something to say, just for the heck of it?" In reply to it, I had just smiled casually.

While sitting in my balcony now, I observed that I was smiling once again, recollecting all this. And, I was asking myself the question, "Where are you going, Arun?"

What you wanted to be –
and –
Where are you going?

Another series of pictures had started reeling in front of my eyes then. Scenes of hostel canteen of my college had come alive to me, when on a chilly winter's night at about 11 pm, I was sitting there with my friends Sanjay, Ashok and Vipin. We were discussing, whether capitalism is good or socialism is fine? We had agreed, that dictatorship is of course bad. "Our people do not deserve democracy", Vipin had just concluded, while finishing his bun and sipping coffee.

Sanjay had visualised a cooperative kind of society – where people collectively put-in their efforts and hard work in fields of their choice, and get their dues proportionately. I was trying then to figure out its feasibility and effects. I had imagined that, indeed it would be a nice idea, if artisans could get right price for their goods, and if fruit-growers would no more need to destroy their fruits like apples, just because of lack of proper transportation and storage facilities.

Ashok had said, "See, what you want and what you get is not always the same. Pankaj wanted to be an artist, but his parents forced him so he joined an engineering college. I am sure, he will never be happy now." I knew he was true. That evening only, I had helped Pankaj to shed-off his suicidal thoughts and to look at life more positively. I knew, Ashok was true in saying, *"Truth is-where you wanted to go and where are you going, is not necessarily matching."*

I was recollecting Ashok's words now, to which I had also added further experiences of fourteen years of my life, since

I had graduated from that engineering institute of international fame.

"*Words are more powerful than a bomb*" – I had read somewhere, and it was applicable to me now, while I was sitting in my balcony in these wee-hours. That flow of words was disturbed when suddenly that whisper again asked me something and these words started exploding aloud in my mind:-

> *What you wanted to be?*
> *Where are you now?*
> *Where are you going?*
> *What do you really want in your life?*

Obviously, I had lived life thus far – full of mismatches, contrasts, contradictions, vanity and vagueness. Worldly, I could have been termed *'successful'* in the eyes of many people. For some, being an engineer and being a government high-ranking officer was an achievement. There were still some who would measure everything in world in terms of money. For them Arun was no extraordinary person, since I wore no extraordinary clothes, did not eat any extravagant food and did not have a lavish, luxurious lifestyle. Well, whatever they thought of me was not significant for me, than what I thought of me?

"*What you think of yourself is more important than what others think about you!*" – is a golden saying.

The pictures I recalled definitely had some contrasts. I was wondering in that silence – What happened of many of our younger days' (of school and college days') dreams, wishes, emotions, desires, aspirations, beliefs and convictions? Why there has been a u-turn – a 180-degree turn in many cases? Is this right or wrong? What are its effects on others and on us? Is this a natural phenomenon? Is it something to do with one's background or one's circumstances? And, after all-why does it happen? What is the remedy? Why should one think of all this?"

All these questions, growing louder in my mind and getting voices, needed answers. I knew I had to think deeper and analyse objectively. I was sure something, somewhere was wrong in all those pictures reeled in my mind then. 'What is it? How to solve it?' was next in my mind....

The whisper which had woken me up, was growing to loud words now, ringing in my mind constantly:

"What you wanted to be? Where you wanted to go? And where are you going now?"...

We are sure-almost all of us at times do think all such issues in life and then we sometimes act on these, sometimes forget. But, these questions owe answers from each of us.

2

A Story Untold: The Journey of Life!

"Change is inevitable, you may only steer its course!"

Dear Reader,

We now welcome you to undertake a mental journey with us.

Just rewind your life mentally some years back, and imagine few such scenarios narrated further. We are sure you do have those sweet memories deep-rooted, down somewhere in your memory lane. May be you do remember such scenarios, or may be some dust accumulated over the years has faded your sweet memories. But we urge you to figure yourself somewhere in these scenarios, which we all encounter in our daily lives.

Surely you will have some thought-provoking session now, and may be you experience a jolt of life.

Preparatory stage: Transitions in past
From where to where you have travelled?

Scene 1: Infancy
(Age–up to 2 years)

Just recall, when you were of age still struggling to express yourself, move around and run as an infant or a child. You sure were amazed and were happy by the sounds of a parrot, a cuckoo and other birds. You felt nice seeing flowers and smelling those. When your father or mother cuddled you up in arms and kissed you on your forehead, you felt on top of the world. When someone gifted you toffees, chocolates or toys, you loved it all.

Life was full of energy. Splashing in water or playing pranks around with your dearest ones was a game of joy. Life was a pleasure and was simple. If you felt hungry you would just cry or make noise and someone would rush to you. If you wanted something and just raise finger and indicate it, and it would be granted.

Wow, how simple it was. Whenever, wherever you wanted, you slept. Whenever, wherever you wanted, you would pee. And if you were in a good mood, laugh aloud. People around you would surely respond to you in a positive manner, either by laughing or smiling with you, or by lovingly looking at you feeling pleasure. Most of the times, you were the centre of attraction in any gathering, like a party etc.

Oh! How wonderful it was. Even now, thinking and recalling it, you would have felt joy.

Scene 2: Childhood
(Age–2 to 12 Years)

(Schooling–Pre-nursery to 8th standard)
Your this world of joy was marred with slight disturbances too, when somebody confined you to four walls somewhere and made you to sit in a chair at a place called – school. You

felt some restrictions, in the name of discipline and learning process. You cried, you created scenes and you threw tantrums at times, in protest. Isn't it? Just try to recollect those scenes. Yes, reading all this itself must be putting a smile on your face while recollecting those days.

You had soon got adjusted to it. It did not dampen your spirits at all. Because, now you had plenty of friends to share your dreams, your aspirations, your emotions. Do you not remember telling your friends something like, "When I will grow up, I will be a_____!" This fill-in-the-blank could be-a pilot, a taxi-driver, a truck-driver, a policeman, a military-man, a doctor, an engineer, a sportsman, a farmer, a businessman, a movie-hero or a heroine…. and so on… The list can grow endlessly with figures you wanted to be.

Just recall yourself talking something like, "When I will grow up I will have_____!" This time fill-in-the-blank could be a big bungalow, an aeroplane, a big car, a big factory, or may be some small things even, which then you might have fancied for.

Also recall yourself saying something like, "When I will grow up I will do_____"! Here the filler could be like – serving parents, taking parents to travel around, charity, seldom a feeling of revenge, or serve people as a doctor, build dams and buildings, do farming etc. How joyous it is to recall all those friends and those shared moments of childhood-dreams and desires.

You wanted to be all that, whatever you thought was related to power, was of significance, was influential and even pleasurable. You wanted to have which could draw attention or give some recognition, which had a show-off value, or which was denied to you at that moment. You wanted to do all that which gave you pleasure, satisfaction, sense of worthiness, praise, blessings, or what you sought as your duty, or you felt as your need.

Basically you wanted to express yourself by way of giving to others, while including your family and friends also in the list of others.

Scene 3:- Adolescence-The Teenage
(Age–13 to 19 Years)

(9th standard of schooling to early years of college)

With schooling, things too became different. You too probably felt changes. If you could sing and murmur at any time earlier as a child, you felt shy now. Like this you have undergone so many changes in you.

Just recollect, small toys did not fancy you any more. You were now interested in sports involving more of running, ball-games, football, cricket, I-spy-you, ludo, carrom, racing etc.

Recall that you had developed certain likings, dislikings, your own tastes, interests, beliefs and aspirations. Whether it was related to choice of food you liked or disliked or was it about your favourite movies, movie stars or heroines. May be it was regarding sports and sport personalities or others around you.

You did like some people and disliked some. May be several of those individuals were your relatives, friends, classmates, teachers or neighbours etc. You liked being in company of some people or aspired to become like them.

You were happy whenever you ate your favourite food or dishes. Certain sports or certain other activities did give you more pleasure.

You were learning some virtues. You liked helping people and sharing whatever you had with others, whom you either loved or felt compassionate for. You liked doing charity or social service. At times, even the activities-like cleaning your school campus, your neighbourhood or your playground collectively – were source of your happiness and satisfaction.

Do you remember yourself uttering some words like, "Oh! Dear, I don't know how will I live without you…" or "You are my best… friend" or "I love … you" or "I will never forget you…" etc. Yes, you had in-fact developed close friendships and relationships with some people. If they are still with you or are around you, you are blessed one.

The interests, beliefs and convictions you developed – you had started expressing through drawing, music, painting, singing, dramatics, debates, letters and poetry or at times merely by talking to some friends or to some people close to you. Your dreams and aspirations were growing strong. You had started seeing an end of the tunnel.

Most of us had even started thinking about issues at state, national or international level. Many of us though were still casual, fun-loving, and merry-go-lucky kind. But some of us had started working for our own dreams, own goals, and ambitions in life.

Just pause... and figure out – where they are today? Most of those early starters have indeed either realised their dreams or are quite near to their goals in life. Isn't it true?

Recapture that you had started to have your own identity, your own personality. People did identify you and gave you compliments like – "Oh Vivek, a really intelligent boy! Oh Asha, a very compassionate girl! Oh Tarun, oh no, he is a selfish boy! Dinesh, Oh what a lovable character he is!....." etc.

All such comments, compliments and feedbacks definitely had their own impact in shaping you further. Recall that, most of your desires, beliefs, convictions, interests, hobbies, aspirations, habits, dreams, and personality traits were infact borrowed, acquired or learnt – either from your parents, brothers, sisters, friends, neighbours, teachers, relatives or from some people who influenced you in life.

Just recollect – what did you dream of having in near future then? May be a good car, home, comfortable life and a happy family. Or may be to travel around. You wanted to be on top of the world. You sought school and college education – for fulfilling your dreams.

You planned to serve your parents, society, and nation by being somebody. May be – a doctor, an engineer, a lawyer, a professor, a farmer, an executive, a soldier or a government officer etc. And then being that, you planned of earning good amount of money, name and fame. You also sought pleasures of life through all these means.

Yah! Definitely it is nice to recollect it all. Some of us might have felt something, while recollecting those sweet memories, those golden dreams and aspirations, which were formed in school and college years.

Some of us wanted name and fame. Some of us wanted to be a great leader, a social worker or a reformist. Someone wanted to be a good artist, a singer, a sculptor, a scientist or a mathematician. Some of us wanted to be an architect – building monuments, an engineer – building bridges and power-houses, or be a mountaineer – scaling heights etc.

Someone, you may recollect now, wanted to do lots of charity or service to society and nation. Someone was a born patriot and wanted to serve motherland by being in armed forces. Yet some another one wanted to be an industrialist, and wanted to create jobs for many others.

Someone wanted to possess all the pleasurable things and luxuries in life. Someone wanted to be an outstanding sportsman. Or may be car racing, cricket, music, tennis, hockey or guitar etc. were passion for some.

Well, so many positive notions and dreams, each of us had. Is it not really refreshing for you to recollect all those early years' desires, dreams and aspirations.

You might sometimes be attaching some pain or some misery, while recollecting all this. And you might be wondering, what is the use? But you need to be patient a little more, to see the points presented in this book, along with the reasons and some remedies suggested.

**Middle Stage: Transitions in present
Phase I
How things change you?
Where you aspired to go?
Adulthood**

(Age-20 to 29 years)
(First 2 to 8 years in your profession)

Let us briefly recall your early years in your respective field of work or your profession, which you might have chosen just after completion of your school or college education. You might be in either a *job* or in a business, or you might have been a self-employed person.

Any professional occupation in service sector where you are your own boss would come under self-employed category. For example being a doctor – doing private practice or running a private nursing home, being a lawyer – doing your own practice, or being an architect, a consultant, a fashion-designer etc. form this category.

Business here means being in fields like – manufacturing, trading, farming, running some shops or showrooms, or being an entrepreneur etc. It means all those areas where you are the employer and you are your own boss. You might have inherited this business or built it your own.

Job means here working for somebody else – either for some individual or for an organisation, a company or government.

The job, business, or self-employment you are in – you might be with your own choice or somebody else might have guided you towards it. Or, may be some circumstances or some individual pushed you or even compelled you into this. You know it best! Anyway, let us quickly recapture memories of those early years in your profession.

Scene 1: Flying High

As a fresh pass-out from school, college or a professional institute, whichever was latest – "What did you think? What did you think you would do? or thought you would get or have? What did you think you would like to become?"

Just recall – "what you thought that world would be like? What had you thought about-how the world, society, or people will respond to you? What were your dreams and your goals then? What was that you desired or wished for at that time? And what were the expectations of yourself and of others around you, from you? What were your own aspirations at that time when you just held that degree, that certificate or got that inheritance?"

Just recollect, the day you got your degree or certificate on completion of your academics from school, college, or professional-institute – you were on top of the world. You did visualise all your beliefs and convictions about academics, making your dreams coming true.

You imagined of a good job – if you chose that – with a handsome amount as pay-package. May be you did get it, may be you did not, or may be you did settle for less. Anyway let us assume you got your dream-job, with all the perks and pay, you imagined then. Wow!

– A beautiful big bungalow! A nice big car! A beautiful or handsome spouse! Or travel around the world with your loved ones! Or doing charity, or helping your nears and dears ones, relatives and others! Etc.

You also thought you would be honest, sincere, hard working, and a person of high morals, values and ethics. Surely you did not imagine all that under the table money or all those soul-killing practices in the first go. Infact you did imagine yourself as someone, who would be contributing significantly to your organisation, your employer, to society and to your nation.

As a self-employed person too, initially you might have picked up a job only. Even if you were daring to directly step into your own venture and you had decided to be your boss – it is fantastic. "What did you imagine then?"

Giving your best services to the world, getting lots of money, getting good name, fame and satisfaction. Did you not visualise all comforts of the world?

Your answer may be either yes or no. But just recollect – "Why did you choose to be on your own or be your own boss?"

Probably because you wanted fast results. You chose to get all you wanted in life by being on your own. You wanted to change lot many things in the world. You sought to change lot many wrong practices around. And you sought to set an example! Was it not so?

You did choose this challenging path as a gateway to cash-on fast the degree or certificate you held. You choose this as a faster vehicle to fulfil your own expectations, your dreams, your aspirations, and also of all those around you.

If you inherited some business, some farmland, some industry, or a shop etc. You were not really dependent on that degree or certificate you held. Fine! But surely when you enter the first time into your inherited business, you too did imagine lot many things. – "What were those?"

"Didn't you see yourself expanding that business leaps and bound?" And, you sought all the pleasures of the world by doing that. Or you saw yourself helping many others by giving them salary, a job, some work. May be you did see yourself as a respected, influential, and a significant person. Or may be you imagined yourself to be a well-recognised person in society and even at national and international level.

"Did you visualise yourself being known and being recognised for unethical, dishonest, wrongful deeds?" – no!

Certainly you had visualised yourself as a respected person known for hard work, imagination, good practices, vision, big and kind heart, and above all as a provider.

You had imagined yourself fulfilling your father, mother, brother, or sister's dream, which could be – expanding that business, or weeding out wrong people. Or may be it was curbing the wrong practices, winning over vices, installing virtues and thus earning respect, satisfaction, name and fame even at national or international map.

Scene 2: Contrasts and Contradictions

Also recollect that soon after you had been in your profession for some time, stretching from few days, weeks, or months to a few years – "what did you find and what did people start telling you?"

You sought unity, but found groupism. You dreamt of integration, but you found divisions based on caste, creed, culture, religion and regional biases etc.

You looked for friendliness, co-operation and joy all around, but you found narrow-mindedness, backstabbing, cribs, complaints and backbiting around.

You wanted to put in your best foot forward, but soon someone came in the way across.

Just recall, "How many times you did hear the unsought advises?"

Something like –
"Be practical",
"All this works in theory only",
"Oh! All this is bookish only",
"Life is not what you think",
"Business is not what you have learnt",
"Co-operate with us",
"Oh! Do not follow ideals",
"Don't have principles",
"Don't take stands",
"Come to real world" etc.!

Or even something like "Do not dream", "Dreams only give pains", etc.

Whatever you had learnt in school and college was soon rejected in real life. Whatever morals, ethics, honesty, sincerity and virtues were imbibed in you, were soon told to be impractical, unrealistic, and un-implementable. You surely felt as if you had learnt nothing so far. There were some definite contradictions and contrasts between whatever you were taught so far and whatever you were forced to unlearn and learn afresh now.

Scene 3: Developments of Cracks

Surely there must have been times in your life when you must have felt disgusted or angry about things you faced. You felt that – why somebody did not tell you the truth?" Or you felt something like – "why don't these people understand you?" These were the first seeds of discomfiture sown in you.

These were the germs of frustration you felt for the first time in life probably. At times you did experience vacuum, a void inside – as if you did not have anybody to whom you could pour out your heart or anyone who could understand you.

You did feel uncomfortable when first time you experienced it. But chances are, soon you reconciled to it thinking it to be a further learning process or some grooming for you.

Wow! Just look back how easily or with how little difficulty you were made to adjust to this kind of mental programming of yours.

As such, you already had a heavy dose, almost an onslaught on you by media, in the form of TV, newspaper, magazines, and movies etc. – all supporting and stressing upon the anarchical and medieval rules like – *'Might is Right'*, *'Revenge is Must'*, *'Lust is all Enjoyment'* etc.

And chances are, that you got accustomed to it all, surely with some pinch of salt initially.

And if you are still different and you are still maintaining your difference, while protecting your identity and originality as well – then you should be congratulated!!

> *It is definitely challenging to stand on your feet amidst fast-speed winds!*

Phase-II:
Where are you heading to?
Rocking of boats

(Age-30 to 40 years)
(Your 8 to 15 years in field)

May be, you as a reader of this story untold, have not reached up to this stage in your real life so far. If not, then we sincerely wish and hope, it does not happen to you what others might have felt or might be feeling in their lives at this juncture. But all you need to do is to take stock of situation now, look at life in a detached fashion and introspect that- "Where have you reached in life so far and where are you heading to now?"

Scene 1: Shattering of Dreams

You will find that perhaps had dreamt of being a good sculptor, a painter, an artist, a stage-performer, a dancer, a singer, a big industrialist, a poet, or a writer etc. Or, you had probably thought to develop something new – may be some new design of bridges, buildings etc. or may be inventing something new. Perhaps you dreamt of being a scientist, an engineer, a doctor, a mathematician, a professor, a teacher, a modern farmer or a journalist etc.

You came into your current profession may be due to some pressures, coaxing, strictures, or comments from your family or society, or may be due to some circumstances. You came in it with your own choice or may be against your wishes.

But, you had still dreamt of having one day some things you always like – a big bungalow with greenery around, a car, lots of money, luxurious lifestyle, beautiful clothes, or any worthy possessions you ever fancied for. You had still nurtured your dream of some day becoming somebody reputed, famous, well-known or a person of eminence, of some stature. You still had dreams of doing great deeds like – charity, inventions, discoveries, creations of everlasting worth, or adventures of life etc.

And – "what did you later find? What did you get or have? What did it start to appear to you? How did you start feeling? What have you been?

You probably felt trapped in your current life and circumstances with all those cherished dreams having started to shatter and your aspirations flying-high getting crushed now.

Isn't it mockery of world you felt, that you are not doing exactly the things or jobs you were cast for? May be a person with mathematical talent is casting dyes, and a sculptor by nature teaches mathematics. May be a person capable and wealthy enough is doing charity running after collections from people. Or may be a person with ability to be an excellent artist is constrained to teach science or work as a clerk.

Here one may find variance in different schools of thought, which we will discuss later. But surely realities rather harsh realities of present environment worldwide, throw numerous challenges to majority of us. We are forced or are limited to have what we do not need, to do that which many of us would never like to do, or to become what most of us never planned to be or ever dreamt to be.

Rising and swimming across the current or tide is not easy for many.

True! Reasons for it can be cited as excessive population, dirty politics, corruption, illiteracy, growing intolerance, growing unemployment and crime, growing insecurity due to fast changing job-scenario and market, government policies or bureaucratic hurdles etc.

But the fact to be examined is one –

Are you pursuing your dreams? Are you happy? Or, are you going to be happy shortly? Even if you say, you are happy and satisfied, check out whether is it really so? Or is it pseudo, self-imposed, transitory and a compromised life?

Scene 2: Changes in thinking

Recollect and look at your life back. Take a minute, pause.... and decide the following.

What changes have taken place in your priorities of life during last 5 to 15 years? What are the changes in your attitudes and in your beliefs – which could be towards yourself, towards others around you or towards world as such? What actions have you been taking or what have you been doing to make your dreams come true? Or have you simply given up?

Just look back – "Has this bug bitten you too?"

That – "Dreaming is bad", "Luck is everything", "Everything is by God's desire only, why to do extra efforts", "Small is beautiful", "Scarcity is comfortable", "Remain contented with little and be happy", "Never think big!" Etc.

Just think – "Is it so with you? Do you subscribe to any of such thing?"

Even if our answer is yes it is alright, and is not your fault. It is what all around you have conditioned you to, in life thus far. But just watch out – "When your neighbour buys a car or a house, do you feel happy or jealous? Or do you go around and tell that he has acquired it in dowry, or by bribe?"

Surely you must have seen such people, who claim to be happy, contented, and satisfied, but always find others at fault. Who seldom praise or appreciate others' achievement of any kind, leave aside celebrate it! Be alarmed! Hope, you are not one of those yet. Reason for saying so would be obvious in the next few paragraphs.

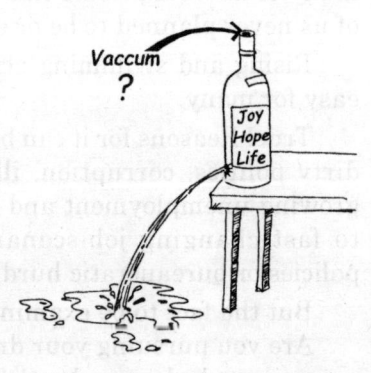

Scene 3: Symptoms of despair

Once a person's attitudes, beliefs and thinking take a downward path, it leads to in-roads of various ailments, diseases and unhappiness.

Stress at work, complaints of overwork and exertion; abuses to boss, spouse and children; a frustrated look and a pale face; various mental, physical, emotional diseases and disorders – all take place with such a person.

Behaviour becomes negative and approach to any work in one's life also becomes negative. You might feel yourself to be in vicious negative loop of life, in such times.

And, slowly but steadily, it leads to various kinds of deterioration-starting with decay of mind which becomes full of worries, tensions, anxieties and fears etc., to decay of body which invites various physical or psychosomatic diseases to disturbed soul and poor finances.

It all ends with unhappy, sadistic personal life, disturbed family life, and uncomfortable periods at work place or profession. Added with it are financial disasters, bad reputation, and ill-fame or disgrace to self and to family.

Abuse of drugs, alcohol, excessive sex, continuous smoking etc. – all compound to one's miseries and troubles.

> And it all leads to vanity in life!

Final Stage
Your Future
A Possibility-
If you don't Wake-Up now!

Scene 1: Where are you going to land?
(Age-41 to about 55 years)

Now, just pause for a minute. Think. Figure out-where are you going to land? View your past and present and think what is going to be your future? If you are already in this age bracket, then just introspect, "What have I become, what have I got, and have done anything of significance so far?"

You had talent, potential and aspirations. You did have talent indeed to excel in any fields of arts or sciences. You did have aspirations to do so many great deeds, so that generations remember you. You wanted to be a really successful person. Name, fame, value, significance, importance, satisfaction, joy, happiness around and luxuries of life were the things you were seeking for. You wanted to *have* all those worthy possessions and assets you sought.

But what are you going to get? What are you going to become? What are you going to do?

Just figure out what is going to happen to you? And in future, what is going to be your health?

- *Mental health.* You are going to be full of fears, worries, tensions, short-temperedness, swollen and shallow ego – all communicable mental diseases.
- *Physical health.* You are going to invite so many physical diseases many of which will be like self-inflicted injuries, directly or indirectly.
- *Emotional health.* With growing intolerance and self-centredness, you are more likely to become a burden, a liability on others-instead of being a *guide* or a *mentor* for youngsters.

- *Spiritual health.* You blame God and your fate all the time for all your failures.
- *Financial health.* You may be broken or may be under huge debts. If you are not then you are shade better. But what will be your total assets and income? How many days or months you are going to survive on that, without doing any work for money?-Barely any. Your income will be just hand to mouth. Because, you never planned your retirement and that retired life for yourself.

Every human being has these five major pillars of *health,* out of which even if any one is weak or is broken, then the whole building of your life is going to crumble down.

Scene 2: Glimpses of your future
Post-retirement life
(Age 56 to about 70 plus years)

Mind controls body is an old saying. But it is true! All sense organs and work-organs are controlled by mind. Just think- what did you dream of and what your attitudes and beliefs are going to be? What is going to happen to your so valuable and important mind?

Surely you may not be lunatic, insane or mentally incapable. But, you may be heading for much worse. Instead of positive-uplifting thoughts you may be thinking more of negative thoughts.

You see accidents and failures first, before positive outcomes. You have fears and worries of failures or of loss, instead of hope for betterment and for success. You feel more of miseries-rather than pleasure, anxiety-instead of calm, confusion-and not clarity!

You do express more of hate and criticism of others instead of *love,* thankfulness and gratitude. You involve yourself more in cynicism, abusing and accusing others, instead of leading, guiding, helping and building others.

And how the society is going to respond to you? All through your life, you thought of society. Thinking like – "What people will say?", "What society will think?", "How my community will respond to me?" Etc. You always thought of all such things, and acted accordingly.

You took many steps, decisions and acted upon those decisions many times dancing to the tune of others, just for society's sake! Even more times you crushed your conscience and your inner-self, just to appease that society. "What will it give to you? Will it really care for you? Can it give you back your dreams?"

May be some individuals will cast their judgements upon you. That too based upon their own skewed perception, their limited thinking, and their narrow view of themselves and of you. That also they do from a distance, avoiding you all together.

"Will that society bother for your mental, physical, emotional, spiritual and financial health? Will anybody be helping you in those areas? Will they help you, in correcting your beliefs and attitudes? Will they solve your worries, tensions, problems and miseries?"

May be representatives and contractors of the same society, for whose sake you spoilt your life and gave up your dreams, will now tell you – "Only you can solve your problems. You only are responsible for your state, you are presently in."

Scene 3: The End
Your obituary!
"Will it be a happy landing?"
Some wise-man has said it nicely – *"How you should live today, can very well be known by just thinking – how would you like your obituary to be read?"* Accordingly you may guide your life then!

True! Just think it deeply for some time –

"Whatever you do today or you will be doing tomorrow; whatever you have accumulated so far or you will have tomorrow, inclusive of all good, bad and ugly; whatever you have become so far or what you will be in the process –

How will it all affect the world once you leave it? How would you like to be remembered as? In what words, people should write and read your obituary?"

A Story Untold: The Journey of Life! ▪ 39

Will it be something like – ?

"Oh, what a great man (or woman)!"

"A man (or woman) of words, of intellect, of character or of a large and kind heart."

"He (or she) was a person of eminence!"

"A person who loved all!"

"A person who always gave to others!"

"A good human being!" Etc.

Also, just figure out –

"How well and how long people will remember you? Will your name go in history – to be remembered forever?"

If you have made a difference around, surely it will.

Surely, you would not like your obituary to be read as following, or people remembering you in following words. Something like –

"A thief!"

"A blood-sucker!"

"A parasite!"

"A selfish-narrow-minded person!"

Or something like – "Oh, very good! At last he (she) has gone!"

Is this what – they are saying about me now? Oh God! I should have known it earlier!

Or, would your obituary be in very simple, cold words? Like –

"Nice person!"

"OK, a good soul! Passed away!" Or

"A poor man (or woman)!" Etc.

May be all along your life, you would have kept on doing all those things, thinking to be your duty, your dharma.

While at the same time you would have kept on ignoring your duties towards your spouse, your children, your parents, and most important of all towards you – yourself!

May be you would have paid the price of it by burning all your cherished 'dreams' alive, by killing all your desires, or by allowing all your talents and skills go down the drain.

But just think –

"What would you get in the end?"

"Would you get, what you wanted or what you still want?"

You wanted happiness, joy, satisfaction, security in life, etc., – "Will you really get it all?"

Think! Even your obituary –

"What you expect it to be and what it would in fact be – do you find them matching or you find these at contrast?"

WOULD YOU LIKE IT ALL?

If your answer to this question is not *yes*, then you must carry-on reading further!

Dear reader,

Look at the picture on the next page and pause here for a few minutes before reading further.

Ask to yourself!

And answer to yourself only!

?

IS THIS YOUR STORY?

Pause here....
Introspect
for some time!

A Story Untold: The Journey of Life • 11

IS
THIS
YOUR
STORY?

Pause here...
Interpret...
In some way.

Part – II

What Went Wrong?

"Nothing is good or bad, only circumstances and environment makes it so!"

Part II

What Went Wrong?

"Nothing is good or bad, only circumstances and our treatment make it so."

3

Is There Any Fault in System Programming?

Perceptions

Let us first consider following few examples to understand some points focused here.

Case 1: Travel by an aeroplane

Suppose you have to travel by an aeroplane from one city to another. While boarding the aeroplane you hear a passenger saying, "This plane's computers may have some fault in system programming!" You know that nowadays in high technology environment, aircraft's onboard computers play a vital role in functioning of its control systems and avionics equipment. If these fail, then the aeroplane is sure shot going to crash.

What would be your reaction now?

If the pilots of the aeroplane tell you the truth that there may be only 10 per cent fault in system programming, still would you fly by the same aeroplane. Even if you were told now that the fault in system programming is not even 1 per cent, would you like to board the aeroplane now?

-No! You would not!

If this would have happened while flying and you had a parachute, you might have even considered jumping out of the aircraft!

Ask yourself now – "Have you checked your system programming? In other words the programming of your system, your mind.

You are not ready to take even one per cent chance with unknown bugs in system programming, while boarding an aeroplane. But how much chances you are taking every day, with so many known bugs in your system's programming?

Consider another example:

Case 2: Journey in a bus

Suppose you have to go to your college, office or your work place in the morning. You are waiting at a bus stand for any bus to come. Imagine, for a long time there is no bus and you are looking at your watch again and again. Suddenly an empty bus comes at a high speed. You feel your pressures

Is There Any Fault in System Programming? ▪ 47

easing out. But just then a passerby announces, "Whoever so wants to travel in this bus, can travel on their own risk. Its engine can fail any time!"

What would you choose then?

Chances are you would mentally calculate things and most probably you would imagine the scenario like this:-

It is probable that you may imagine yourself getting delayed for your college, office or your work place etc. and you might even consider boarding that bus. However, the moment you imagine the scene of its engine failure, perhaps you would prefer to let go that bus and wait for another one.

But what about your mental engine? Are not you in the bus whose engine might have failed you several times due to faults like – errors of judgement or wrong perceptions, leading you to wrong destinations? It may be even preventing you from reaching your full speed-your full potential.

Consider one more example now:

Case 3: Horse-riding

Assume you are an excellent horse-rider. Riding on a horse is your passion. One day while doing your morning jog, you see a beautiful, strong, white horse. You go near it, pat its back and put your hands around its neck. The horse behaves gently, and responds lovingly to your strokes. You are really tempted to take a short ride on this horse. Suddenly, someone comes near you and says, "Hey, do you know, this horse can go insane anytime? You should be staying away from it."

What would you do then?

Chances are, you would drop the idea of riding on that horse, and would somehow console yourself.

An after-thought

In all these cases considered above, if you happen to be a daredevil kind, then it is good. You are brave. It also exhibits your rationality. But, for most of the people what really happens is the issue. That perception is the point of focus here.

Observe the difference in perception now.

Consider these facts:
- There is no aircraft's computer in the world, which does not have absolutely any bug in its system programme! How so ever small probability of failure it may have, but it exists in all aeroplanes of the world.
- There is no engine of any bus in the world, which never fails. Every engine of every bus has to fail, some time or the other.
- Any horse in the world anywhere, can go insane any time in its life. There is no certainty that it would not.

Now if you consider these facts deeply, you would probably laugh aloud on yourself. You would probably like to reprogramme yourself now.

The Fault!

Think this question for a while:

"What really happened in all three examples above?"

You will answer perhaps –

"Perceptions! Programming of Mind!!"

Someone along the line of life just skewed your perceptions and programmed your mind in some wrong way.

That you need to check in your life too.

"Is everything all right with your mind? Is there any fault in your system's programming?"

By faulty programming of *mind* and still not correcting it, what happens in life, would be more evident from the following popular story.

A Story : Punditji and Four Thugs

There was a punditji (a Hindu priest) living in a town. He was a man of intellect and wisdom. People used to address him as punditji, in respect for his knowledge, wits and age.

He was a middle-aged average-built man living within his average income. For his livelihood punditji used to go to houses of people and perform rituals on various occasions, tell them *kathas* (religious stories) and preach. People in return used to give him either things in kind or in cash. And punditji used to live happily on that.

One day, punditji was invited for naming-ceremony of a child. After the ceremony was over, he was donated a calf, some money and clothes by the host.

The punditji was happy and he was imagining his future on his way back! – "I will feed this calf nicely, it will grow up. When it will grow up, it would be a cow, which will give me milk and further calves. I will drink milk and also sell it. Those calves also would grow up as some cows and bulls. I will now sell bulls and will also sell more milk. Oh! My life would be changed then. I am going to be a rich man. Wow! God, you have been very kind to me today."

Thus, the punditji was walking, thinking, imagining and day-dreaming while carrying that cute little calf on his shoulders, all along the way back to his home.

There were four *thugs* (baddies), watching him from a distance, while standing behind a tree. The cute little calf tempted them. But they did not wish to snatch it from a priest and annoy God! So, they thought of a trick to grab that calf from him.

They placed themselves at one-mile distance each along the path of Punditji. The first *thug* then meets the punditji and after greeting him *namastey* he says, "Punditji, you are a wise man. I respect you for that. But why are you carrying a dog on your shoulders?" At this the punditji smiled and replied, "Check your eyes. It is a calf." And, he continued walking, thinking, 'what kind of crazy people are in this world?'

After a mile, the second *thug* meets the punditji. He also wishes him and says, "Punditji, You are a man of great intellect! But tell me-why are you carrying a donkey on your head?" Punditji was quite amazed now! Anyway, in low voice he replied, "No, it is a calf." And he continued his journey to his home.

Another mile, and the third *thug* meets him now. He too greets the punditji and says, "Punditji, everything is alright. But what will you do of a goat? Its milk will upset your stomach and smell your mind too." Now the Punditji was really taken aback. He was disgusted now. He replied, "What's happened to you all? Somebody sees it as a dog, someone a donkey, and yet another one a goat! Have you all gone crazy? Oh! It's simply a calf."

Is There Any Fault in System Programming? ■ 51

But now the punditji was quite perplexed! He started having self-doubt too. – "Have all these chaps I have met so far gone crazy or something is wrong? Am I wrong? What is the matter?"

It was falling dark now. Slowly he walked, pushing himself forward in disgust, when the fourth *thug* draws his attention by greeting him. He says, "Punditji, I never expected you to act in such a foolish way. Why the hell on earth, you are carrying a dead fox on your head? Shameful!"

Now the punditji was scared too. He just dropped the calf there and ran. He ran, as if he was running for his life, till he reached his home. He did not even look back.

All the four thugs assembled, took the calf with them and walked back to their homes, laughing to their glory.

Well! Check yourself – "Do you also behave like punditji in your life?" – allowing your system to be programmed faultily by others, then dance to their tunes and suffer throughout your life.

4
What is Malfunction in the System?

We all human beings live on air (oxygen), water and food. We get nourishment, health, energy and growth by these. We all eat food. Agreed? But what kind of food do we eat.

Junk food

Suppose if you start eating junk food (so called fast food) daily at least twice a day or at all your three meals of the day!

May be you are consuming foods like noodles, *chana bhaturas, pakoras, chats,* pizzas, *dosa, pao-bhaji,* omelettes or *bhel-puri,* chicken, fish etc. at all time and on daily basis.

"Then what will happen?"

– Sooner or later your stomach would be upset and health would go down. -That would be your answer! Isn't it?

If you say, "yes" – then all right!

Your answer is perfectly all right. You are stating a *truth* only!

You mean, "By feeding junk-food to your stomach, at all meals every day – it would get upset. It would start malfunctioning. Your energy levels would reduce drastically. And you would be required to take appropriate medicine to cure it. You would also be advised by the doctor treating you, to correct your eating habits also."

O.K.! Ask yourself now –

"What are you feeding to your brain, to your mind?"

You know, your mind controls your body. And if your body (i.e. your stomach) is fed junk food regularly, then –

What is Malfunction in the System? ▪ 53

What would happen to your mind, which is being fed junk food only, at all times?

What do you feed to your mind throughout the day?

Yes! You need to look back into your daily life and introspect.

"What do you feed to your mind, daily, right from morning till night?"

In the morning you get up late, and feed news to it – through newspaper, TV or radio.

54 ■ Wake-Up Call in the Wee Hours

Though all these mostly contain negative talks only –

So many rapes, murders, thefts, riots accidents, loot, terrorist-attacks, wars or suicides etc.; so and so politician or bureaucrat criticised so and so; X abused Y; Y's crib is this and that; A threatened B etc.

Then you proceed to your work place.

First buses, local trains or autorickshaws give you a good lousy welcome to begin your day – if you are not commuting by your own vehicle. Drivers, conductors or some nagging and crying co-passengers also pollute your mind enough, adding pollution on roads.

Then you reach at your work place. There too all the bad events of the previous day are discussed first. Criticism of boss, colleagues, and their spouses or of own spouse even, follows next.

In the evening when you come back home – your spouse, your children, may be parents or others living under same roof with you are all too eager to share their day's events with you. But unfortunately mostly negatives only.

A session of cribs, complaints, abuses, critics and fault finding with others begins.

Your colleagues, boss, spouse's colleagues, relatives, friends, neighbours, kids' teachers and their school or college-mates etc. all are roped in.

At night you and your family spend time religiously with a well-known idiot box TV'. There again most of your favourite serials, soap operas and movies, feed mostly all negatives, vices and critics only, to your mind. All this is fed to your mind along with a heavy dose of commercials and advertisements, most of which are tall claims only.

The next day morning, another such cycle starts once again.

So –

"What has been fed to your mind throughout the day? And what will be the effect of it all on your mind?"

What is Malfunction in the System? ■ 55

The Malfunction

Even computers have two kinds of memory. FIFO and LIFO-*First In First Out* and *Last In First Out* respectively.

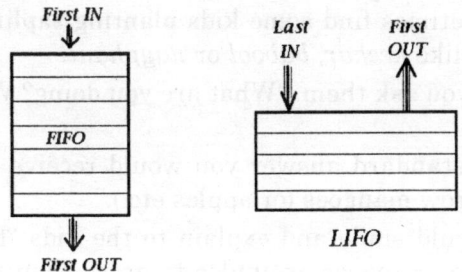

Whatever has been fed in as input, so will be the output. Similar is the case with your mind.

"You reap what you sow!" It is an old saying. But it is very much applicable even till date and in all walks of life.

Your mind, your *system* works purely on GIGO *principle*.

The Gigo principle is –

Garbage In, Garbage Out!

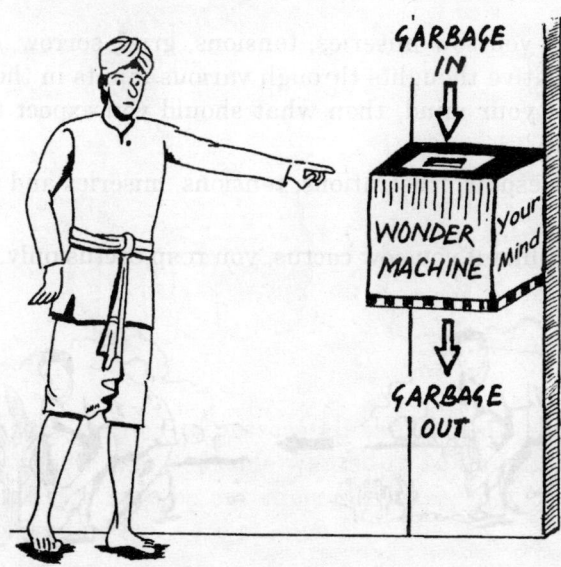

Yes! – If you feed garbage to your mind, garbage fills it and garbage only comes out of it!

That is the malfunction in the system.

As a child you might have done it yourself, or even now you might sometimes find some kids planting saplings of some wild plant like *keekar*, *babool* or *nagphani*.

When you ask them, "What are you doing? Why are you doing it?"

– The standard answer you would receive is, "We are trying to grow mangoes (or apples etc.)."

You would smile and explain to the kids "Look, if you want maize, mangoes or apples to grow, then you need to plant those very saplings only. *You reap what you sow!*"

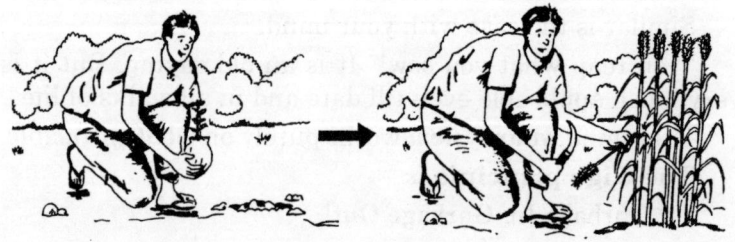

So if you sow miseries, tensions, grief, sorrow, despair and negative thoughts through various inputs in the fertile lands of your mind, then what should you expect to grow and reap?

– Despair, frustrations, tensions, miseries and worries only.

Just like-if you sow cactus, you reap cactus only.

What is Malfunction in the System? ■ 57

Yes! That is why you get what you have. That is why you do what you do. That is why you are what you are.

"Good, bad or ugly-whatever shades of grey you are, you are. Absolute white or absolute black is seldom possible!"

What decides your destiny?

Whatever you feed to your body, mind and soul, so are the outcome as the results of it! That only decides your fate. That only decides your destiny added with action – the effort level.

But here is a big difference. Only human beings are endowed with such powers by nature that they can control the inputs.

Only human beings are capable of checking inputs, ingredients, and quality of things fed to their body, mind and soul. Animals are not given this power by nature.

So, why not make the best use of this unique power of discretion bestowed upon you?

"Control your inputs, your outputs will also be favourable"

And that would decide your destiny.

5

Myths Created

"A myth is a slow poison to society and human mind!"

Myths

People with some vested interests or people having negative minds, at some point of time in the history of human kind have created some myths too.

These myths are prevalent in almost all societies, countries and religions. These are too deep-rooted in all classes of people, of all ages, sex, economies and strata.

These myths have also hampered and retarded one's growth significantly at times. These have also prevented people from realising their true potential.

A correct understanding of various common myths widespread in our country, in the light of wisdom, is the best solution in itself towards dispelling these myths.

Common Myths

Myth 1
'Ignorance is bliss!'

It is a very strong-rooted and widespread myth, which you must have heard or encountered several times in your life so far in all walks of life. Surely in India at least.

"Can darkness dispel darkness?" no! *"Light only dispels darkness!"*

"Ignorance is Bliss", yes! But for fools only!

Recollect the well-known story of *Kalidas* in India, who happened to be cutting the tree's branch on which he was sitting! Till wisdom dawned on him, he was considered a fool only.

Just think – if you believe in this myth then – "who would be at loss?"

So you should always complete the sentence in your mind whenever you hear – *"Ignorance is Bliss"* – as – *"But for fools only, not for wise!"*

"Wisdom is true bliss! Feigning ignorance is foolish!"

Myth 2
'Death solves all miseries!'

It may be true built it is only the apparent view.

Just think – "Are you a believer or an atheist?"

If you were a believer then "how come death would solve all your miseries? Your those miseries would be felt even by your small body, the causal body, and not only by you yourself in your next birth."

If you were an atheist then – "if you would not have life at all, how will it matter to you, whether you had miseries or not – for you would not be experiencing it!"

Think – "How death can be a solution to life?" – It cannot be.

Only life is solution to life! Therefore, Live Fully!! Living fully solves miseries, not death.

Myth 3
'Less is enough! Small is beautiful!'

If you subscribe to this myth, do one thing –

You may choose to be generous, ask your employer or your customer to pay you less.

Would you like it then?

Or you may do another thing-shift your office or residence and move with your family to an accommodation, which is not even 50 per cent in area and comforts than you previously had.

How would you like it? How would your family members like it? Would you still believe 'Less is enough! Small is beautiful!

Surely, you would say "Nonsense! Not always!"

It must be understood that, these words are myths – some pseudo beliefs created by those few narrow minds, who had small or no dreams and who always have got little only but achieved nothing.

This myth was created probably as a justification of non-performance, non-achieving and pseudo-satisfaction only.

Therefore believe that –

Big is beautiful! More only is enough.

"Abundance and not scarcity is the key!"

Myth 4
'Be satisfied. Do not try further!'

It is a big misnomer. Two meanings are possible here of the first half of these words. It is a big myth if interpreted as – 'be satisfied, and you should not put in any efforts to try anything further.' That is what most people interpret it as, and they never do anything extra and in turn they do not get anything extra.

"Extraordinary efforts and extraordinary actions only bring extraordinary results."

Correct interpretation of this phrase 'Be satisfied' is, when it is interpreted as – "Do your best efforts, then be satisfied with whatever comes to your store!"

Yes! That makes sense! But here too, the first half line is more important- as you put in "your best efforts!" and not casual efforts.

Naturally, once you first put in your best effort in something, you would get desired results most of the time. And by some reason if the results are not as expected then do not be frustrated, and 'be satisfied with whatever you get and continue to strive for better outcomes in future.'

That is the spirit required. That is the correct meaning here.

Myth 5
'All is luck!'

Again, this phase has a double meaning. If the interpretation is – 'you cannot get what is not there in your luck!' – then ask yourself – "How would you know, whether 'something' is there in your luck or not, until unless you try it hard? May be, 'something' is stored in your luck and you are not trying at all to get it!"

How would you know?

Also – "What is luck? Who makes it? What shapes it?"

"If luck is governed by *'prarabdha'*, your past deeds, then you govern it and you make it!" Again, it means – "Your actions make your luck!"

Therefore another interpretation, which should correctly be taken and be understood, is –

"Put-in your all-out efforts. Take all actions and measures. Then whatever is obtained as results, take that in to stride, accept that as given by your luck, as your dues to you, according to your past deeds."

> Your past *made* your present!
> Your present *would make* your future!!

That is what scriptures also teach.

Solution

Therefore this fault in your system programming, this malfunction in your system, in the form of your negative programming, is caused by these widespread and deep-rooted five myths.

These need to be erased and need to be deleted not only from your mind but from majority of other minds too.

The only possible *solution* you seem to have is that –

You have to replace these five myths, with correct programming, by your own positive-programming words or by the positive-programming words of five facts suggested on the next page.

Negative Programming: 5 Myths

1. Ignorance is bliss!
2. Death solves all miseries!
3. Less is enough! Small is beautiful!
4. Be satisfied. Do not try further!
5. All is luck! You can get more, so do not try, and do not put in efforts.

 Replace these with

Five positive-programming facts

1. Wisdom only is bliss!
2. Living life lively solves miseries!
3. Abundance, not scarcity is the key! Big is beautiful!
4. Do your best efforts, then be satisfied with whatever you get!
5. Your actions make your luck! You can control your future!

6

Misplaced Priorities and Wrong Programming

We have set priorities in life. Every activity we do, every event, which takes place in human life, has some set order. That only brings order and certainty in this world. The following few examples would amply clarify what happens when we upset it even a bit.

Misplaced priorities

Case 1: Dinner in a garden-restaurant

Imagine you go to a restaurant, to relish a three-course meal. Imagine you are having a romantic evening with your spouse, a date, close friend or someone you love.

A good soft music is being played and you are really having a good time.

After some time a waitress brings you an ice- cream or the dessert you had ordered.

Then she brings some *sounf, paan, supari* etc. Then she serves you all the dishes you had ordered, and lastly the soup.

Misplaced Priorities and Wrong Programming ■ 65

Yes! She serves you all the things as per your order only but has just jumbled the set sequence, the priorities a little. How would you like it then?

Case 2: Dressing-up for a party

Imagine you are taking bath and you have to go to a certain party. Someone, may be your beloved knocks at the bathroom-door and asks you to hurry up. In the hurry, you first put on the suit, followed by some shirt and trousers. And then you put on your undergarments.

Can you visualise yourself in such a state, showing yourself up at the party?

Can you imagine the funny scene?

How would it look to you?

All just because of misplaced priorities, while putting on the clothes.

These are just couple of examples from real life, where priorities get hotchpotch and just a small change of order can create some real-scenes.

What happens if you have misplaced priorities in life?

It would be like:

- Instead of working for yourself, you work for somebody else.
- Instead of making your dreams come true, you work for realising somebody else's dreams.
- Instead of exploring your potential and nurturing your talent, you become just a puppet in somebody else's hands.

Result of misplaced priorities in your life

When you fail to realise, what should be given priority in life by you, and what should not be? Then what does happen and what can happen to you, to your life. It is something like the result depicted in the next example.

Case 3: Travelling in a luxury car

Imagine you are travelling in a chauffeur-driven, air-conditioned and luxurious car, listening to some nice music.

You ask the driver for an ashtray. Suddenly you see a fast approaching truck on the collision path to your car. You immediately warn your driver. But your driver, first switches off the music, then switches off the air-conditioner, and then he would give you the ashtray.

After, all this only, he tries to manoeuvre the car by steering it sharp.

Imagine, what will happen?

> *"Misplace the priorities in life,*
> *and* the results *will all be* misplaced *too!"*

Wrong programming

Not only do we have skewed perceptions, wrong inputs to mind, various myths and misplaced priorities in our lives, but a lot other wrong-programming is also fade into majority of our minds. This wrong programming is done in our subconscious and conscious minds both – by various sources. This might have been done intentionally or even unintentionally.

What is wrong programming?

Human body has sense organs and work organs, which is controlled by mind or rather call it brain.

"What controls these?"

The nervous system commands and controls our mind over our body. That is why the mind is always given higher priority than body.

It is something like supervisor (or manager) vs worker.

If this supervisor lacks control over its worker – our body – then the result is paralysis.

If this supervisor, this manager is filled with dirt, wrong notions and beliefs, imagine – Would workers deliver their best? – Never.

So is the relation of the human mind and the body.

"If your mind is fed, filled or cluttered with some wrong notions, myths and wrong beliefs-that is wrong programming."

For e.g., in your childhood you must have been told at times by your grandma, your grandpa or by others – about some particular house, corner or some shady area – in various strange words. "Don't go near to it. If you go there, some ghost, satan, or some devil will harm you etc."

It must have been told to you without any ill-design or any ulterior motive. It might have been told to you, just to scare you or just to divert your attention sometimes. And then, you used to be scared by not only that particular spot, but all such similar spots gave you shivers all through your life then onwards.

Just recollect, how bad you had felt when you grew up and found that no such thing existed there. All those years you were simply fooled.

This is a very common example of wrong programming, which might have been experienced by majority of us in life.

Such negative programming kills one's creativity and also affects one's potential.

Who does this wrong-programming?

Like the old saying that – *"Charity begins at home"*, things start at home only.

Most of the times, parents and family members – brothers and sisters etc. also do this negative programming – may be inadvertently.

This is further strengthened by your teachers at schools and later at colleges.

It is further reinforced, as if adding fuel by society around you-your friends, neighbours and relatives.

And when you grow up the society, government, media like – TV, newspapers and movies, your most of the bosses and colleagues at work and even your organisation itself, do put-in the left-over nails in the coffin box of your creativity and potentiality.

Why one does it?

You might be wondering – "Why would anybody do that, the negative programming to you? What could be the motive behind? What would one *achieve by it?*"

Well, the reasons to do so, by people could be unintentional or may even be intentional.

Unintentional reasons

Unintentional reasons of doing a wrong programming by people, could be their own ignorance, their own wrong notions, wrong beliefs, overprotection to you and their fears.

It could also be their lack of awareness, their limited, small-narrow thinking, or may be their shortsightedness.

Intentional reasons

But there could also be a few intentional reasons of some people, behind doing wrong programming of yours.

These may be like jealousy, unhealthy competitiveness, fears of your success or their inferiority complex arising due to their own incompetence.

Misplaced Priorities and Wrong Programming ■ 69

In case of organisations and governments – reasons may simply be dominance and governance.

How wrong programming is done?

Most common forms of wrong programming done to you by various sources can be summarised in the following words.

Your wrong programming is done mostly either by telling you these words verbally or by drilling these words into your psyche by use of any verbal, written means or any audio-visual-print media available.

"How many times in life you have heard, or have been told or have come across, either of these following ten major wrong programming phrases?"

Wrong programming words

1. You cannot do it. Or I can't do it.
2. Do not have dreams. Or never dream big.
3. Are you a hero? Or don't try to be a hero.
4. Always follow the crowd. Or follow the trend or current. Or be a mediocre always.
5. Don't try to beat the system or organisation.
6. You cannot change! You can't change – yourself, things or the system.
7. It has to be done this way only.
   Don't try to change the track.
8. Do not think.
9. Boss is always right.
10. Maturity comes by age, by grey-hairs.

You must eradicate these wrong programming words from your life.

Introspect! Also check – "Are you doing it further to others?"

Think! Recollect – "Who told you so? Who said those words to you?" Why one would have told you so?" Or, if you yourself are doing it to others now, then analyse- "Why are you saying so to others? What is your motive?"

Finally-think over the following:
- Should you listen to it?
- Who's at loss? And
- Should you be doing it?

Beware! Wrong programming to mind is deadlier than poison! Avoid it!

Suggested solution

Awareness, vigilance and self-introspection are the keys. Whenever somebody tells you something, it may not necessarily Gospel truth. It may be wrong. Check whether it is any kind of wrong programming? Compare it with the list of those ten above.

If your answer of findings is yes, then reject *it* straightaway. Do not allow it to enter your mind. You can always control what you feed to your mind.

Also, if you happen to be doing it yourself to others or to your children, in any way – "Stop right away."

"Words are mightier than sword!"

7

The Wee-Hours!

Change

These are the changing times – challenging and tough. Any change has its plus and minus aspects both! Every gain involves risk! A simple theory- *"No risk, no gain! As much risk, as much gain!"* can be applied in any walk of life.

Change only, brings gain. But change also brings challenges. These challenges may be tough at times. If you are prepared emotionally, mentally and physically to meet those challenges and other demands of change, you definitely stand to gain.

"Change is eternal truth of nature!"

Everything changes in this world, with every fraction of time.

Your ideas, your health, your desires and dreams, your surroundings, your friends, relatives or near and dear-ones, your income or expenditures and economy, your thinking, beliefs and attitudes, your habits, choices, likes and dislikes etc. – anything – nothing remains static.

Haven't these undergone any changes in past 5 years, or in past 5 months, 5 hours, 5 minutes, or even in past 5 seconds?

Your answer would be 'yes'! They have changed.

Scientifically too – the global position of stars, planets, sun, earth and moon etc., – all objects the astrologers believe in, and astronomers study, change their position. And, so is their effect on human beings, if you believe in the science of astrology.

With every fraction of a second, every electron of every atom of every molecule of every particle of every thing in this universe is changing its form and position. This causes change.

"Can you resist change? Can you stop it? Can you allow it not to happen?" Then "how can you think of and afford to remain static?"

A perspective

There was a memorable movie of a famous actor of Hindi films Raj Kapoor. In this movie, in a scene, he happens to perform *Sheersha-Asana* at seashore. (*Sheersha-Asana* is a *yoga asana*, in which one stands on head with both feet up in the air vertically.)

A passer-by sees him like this and asks in amazement, "Hey! What are you doing? Why are you standing like this up-side down?" to which, the character depicted by Raj Kapoor replies, "Friend, this whole world is *ulta* (of opposite nature), so I am just trying to align myself to it, to see it in a correct way."

Wow! What a perspective?

Well, moral of the story is not that you too need to perform that sort of physical movement. But if you want to see the world in correct fashion and live winning over it, you will have to align yourself first to see it in its correct perspective. And that would require you to change your outlook.

The chaos: The dark clouds
In these changing times, one witnesses chaos everywhere.

Jobs are getting unpredictable, short-term and scarce owing to frequent economic-recessions, slow-downs and job-layoffs running millions in number, throughout the world.

Unemployment is growing with unpredictable scenarios at industries – be it private sector, multinationals or public sector undertakings.

With public sector and other private companies' sell-offs and mergers, the job opportunities, profits in shares, dividends, and share markets all remain unpredictable and unstable.

Lab problems are on the rise in industries. Employees switch jobs more frequently nowadays.

In addition to reducing loyalty of staff, changes in trade-policies of government or changes in worldwide trade laws and practices, pose grim pictures and present difficult times ahead, for business and industry sector, both.

Ever-surmounting corruption, violence, materialism, lust of sex, and terrorism worldwide are definitely scaring for anyone.

74 ▪ *Wake-Up Call in the Wee Hours*

Increased competition with foreign goods due to various factors, and tough global competition are forcing us to live more of machine-life.

Merger of crime with politics, growing erosion of morals, values and ethics from all walks of life, and growing organised criminal and terrorist activities – these with all other above factors cast dark shadows of wee-hours on human life.

Short-term gains and personal interests are gaining priority over all social, national, international and human issues etc.

– All these can be cited as numerous factors responsible for growing unrest, disturbance, insecurity, fears and lack of courage in every human mind.

One definitely gets an impression of dark clouds, hovering over our present times and over our future as well.

Future does appear bleak indeed.

How does this chaos around relate to you?

In these challenging times presently, the roads into future also do not give any ray of hope especially for those who have been programmed by various people and by various

Three Types of People ▪ 75

influencing factors throughout their life's journey so far. For all the people who strongly believe-in and live by morals, virtues, ethics, sincerity, honesty, integrity and hardwork etc. – life is really tough, full of challenges, and full of thorns all along the way.

- For the people who dream of ever being something or doing something for their own satisfaction or for the sake of society, country, or human race as a whole;
- For the people who ever have been or still are alive by heart or mind or by both;
- For the people who do have the desire and potential to excel in any field of either arts or sciences;

For all such people both the present and future-times are definitely challenging and raise less of hopes rather more of difficulties in the path.

While treading your upright path, may be you are facing it presently or you might have faced in the past – various adversities like-stiff opposition, suppression, ridicules, temptations, allurements, tricks, threats of elimination, critics and condemnation etc.

If you happen to belong or at-least support this class of people-then you need to be congratulated.

You are the one we are searching for.

A question in wee-hours!

When *the present* is so tough and challenging, and the future is so bleak-then the obvious question is –

"In these wee-hours, what should one do?"

A famous Urdu poet of India has also expressed it like this:-

"Junoon ka daur hai, kis-kis ko jayen samjhane!
Kuch yahan bhi akal ke dushman, kuch wahan bhi deewane!!"

Means-

"These are the times of craziness! Whom all people we can attempt to explain and make them understand?"

"There are some people around you, running short of wisdom, and here in this side of world too are some crazy people!!"

Well, there is also the old saying –

Thus introspect and evaluate yourself –

Are you ready, yourself first?

To look for the way-out and to have first a required understanding of the process involved so that you can overcome the dark clouds in these wee-hours.

Part – III

Understand the Process!
"What you have not been taught in schools and colleges?"

> *"Every effect in the world has some cause behind!"*
>
> If you want to change your future, influence your destiny, make your dreams come true and towards it all, even if you want to change yourself – in order to change your present – then the first step you need to take is to understand the process involved.
>
> You need to first understand, what goes into and what is behind all actions and responses of human beings, and why?
>
> A clear understanding of these aspects only, can bring one to a stage when he or she is ready to learn- 'how should I go about it now'?
>
> Therefore it is appropriate that we discuss first the various processes involved at this juncture and then revisit these time-to-time.

8

Three Types of People

All people in society, in country and in the whole world around you can be divided into three categories depending on their thinking and attitudes.

Category 'A' people: want everything, do nothing!

These are the people who have wishes, desires and may be some dreams too. These people do want everything in life. All worthy possessions-be it a big house, a bungalow, or a big car, or a luxurious lifestyle, or-may be name, fame and legacy etc. are their wishes.

If you ask them directly – "do you want it... more? What are you ready to do for it?" Then you would get either of the two responses. Either the person would say, "I am happy, I am satisfied, I do not want anything more!" Or the person would say, "Yah! Fine! It's O.k. with me, if I get it... But I can't do anything for it! You know, I have this... this...and that... problems!"

People who claim or pose to be happy and satisfied, if they are really so in reality and not pseudo, then it is good. Because, that is what everybody seeks for in life. These people deserve to be saluted.

But here is a caution. It should not be pseudo! It should not be self-imposed. Many people would claim to be happy and satisfied, with what they have got, and with whatever present state they are in. But in reality inside their heart they are not. They may be neither happy nor satisfied.

There is a test for such people – when any of their friend, neighbour, relative, colleague or competitor either buys a new house, a new car, motorbike or scooter or one acquires any other symbol of luxurious life, or one gets some award, some recognition etc.-then what emotions are generated in these people? How do they react to it? Do they say something like "Oh? That chap! You know he has got it in dowry!" Or may be something like – "He or she has got that recognition by unfair means, by licking only." Etc.

Just think now would a person truly satisfied and happy from inside, comment and condemn others' achievements, howsoever small it may be, in such manner? The answer would be no.

There are some other kinds of people also in this category. People who want everything, but they are convinced in their mind and also try to convince others that they could not do anything. If you tell them any solution steps then they would cite hundred problems in each step.

These are the people, who have clung to their present mould so much that they do not want to even step outside of their comfort zone. They will show all inabilities or the reasons of their not putting-in any efforts in different words as if "their health is not O.K., they are too busy, they have liabilities or social commitments. They are not trained, they lack required skills or knowledge and they are not really cut for it. They have neither time nor money, they just cannot do it, or they are not smart enough. They are born in a wrong family, society or country. Their parents, family members or society are bad, so is the government or administration. Their luck is bad too etc."

Such people quote numerous reasons for not progressing, for not advancing, or for not achieving anything in life. Yet they want it all. Therefore frustrations, cribs, complaints, crying, nagging, criticising and blaming others etc., fill their days and life. These poor people live life like those earthworms lying in a drainage, who keep on hustling, bustling and jolting others, but ever remaining where they were, where they are.

"They want, but they can't!"

"They want, but they wouldn't try anything!"

These are the people, who always look forward to some miracles happening to them. They keep waiting throughout their life, for some magic, some miracles, some sudden bout of good luck, etc. They believe in lotteries and in prize-winning TV shows, etc., without even realising how others are making money at their cost. Such people want quick bucks which is rarely there. They believe in fate strongly. And want to play safe, no risks.

They need to realise some fundamentals of life that – **"One has to make magic or miracles happen, only then you can influence your luck."**

"Whatever you have got today, is the result of what you sow in your past. Whatever you would sow today, would yield results."

"No risk, no gain!

As much risk, as much gain!"

"Even plants, birds or animals do not get anything, without putting in some efforts first!"

Category 'B' people: want everything, take shortcuts!
There are people who want everything in the world to possess and have for them alone. All luxuries and comforts of life are their first and foremost desires. They want all materialistic things. People in this category want to have it all – a good house, a big car, a luxurious lifestyle, world tour,

entertainment, a good school or college for the education of their children, etc. *They want everything-but they do not want to 'earn' it by their own.*

They resort to shortcuts most of the times and adopt unfair, unethical, illegal and immoral ways like taking commissions, bribe,

undue favours and gifts from people they oblige in their lawful capacity, or taking dowry etc.

Deep inside, these people too are driven by motivation of uplifting their living standard and their present status. They want to improve their present and their future. But they develop some pseudo-beliefs early in their lives, mostly by being influenced under some such few forces, which programme their mind and which propagate that – 'this path though is immoral, unfair, and illegal but is shortest.'

Invariably these people do have good potential, intelligence and capability, which they put to use for personal petty gains through unfair and shortcut means.

What a miss? How foolish?

People in this category, fail to understand and realise few important aspects in their lives.

First of all, they do have potential through which they can fulfil all their dreams just by tapping their dormant, hidden energies and unexplored capabilities.

Secondly, they never would be at peace with themselves and never would they lie in comfort and grace, if they resort to unfair means.

Moreover, their own 'guilt-conscience' would not allow them to really enjoy, whatever they seem to enjoy this way.

Category 'C' people: want everything! increase self-potential and achieve it!

People, who belong to this category, too have dreams and goals. They too are mostly driven by motivation of having more. They also want everything in life. Their domain of their wants is even larger than that of any of previous category people.

These people want not only materialistic things like luxuries and comforts, but they also want many other intangibles like good, balanced, health, name, fame, legacy and doing charity etc.

But, their philosophy of life is –

"Want more, work more", or "Want more, get more degrees and stamps on themselves." Or, "Want more, do more."

People in this category do believe in maximising their natural gifts, increasing their acquired skills and knowledge, putting more hard work, tapping their own potential and in increasing their own competence level.

They believe in making their own line bigger!

People in this category also continue putting-in their efforts, believing that – "Right education and more hardwork will fetch them more."

They are not wrong. But they need to understand some more facts of life. With 'hard-work' they need to do more of 'smart-work' too.

They definitely need more 'education', but not merely 'degrees'.

All these points are discussed in further chapters.

But definitely, belief of these people that
- by thinking more and big,
- by increasing and maximising self-potential,
- by increasing their competence level, and then
- by raising their effort-level, they can have more

That is exactly what happens in life.

Which category of people you belong to?

Now take a break! Pause! Introspect! Think and decide- "Which category of people you belong to? – A, B or C?"
- *Category 'A' person-* will never get, what one wants.
- *Category 'B' person-* may get, what one wants, but it would be short-lived.
- *Category 'C' person-* will not only get what one wants, but it would be long lasting too.

Category 'C' is one, where the challenge lies, where one gets not only luxuries and comforts but where 'intangibles' of greater importance are also obtained in life. Intangibles as name, fame, reputation, legacy, true self-satisfaction, meaningfulness, fulfilment, joy and glory etc.

A fact!

"Every person deep inside his or her heart, mind and conscience belongs to category C of people."

"It is only a question of environment one is subjected to, conditioning of mind by others and by self, thinking and attitudes of one self, and effort-level one puts-in."

Therefore, if you belong to *Category 'C'* – it is fantastic. But even if you belong to category 'A' or 'B' presently is not a problem.

You can change yourself, your present, and influence your destiny.

You can switch over to category 'C' and you can succeed in life as well just by –
- changing consciously your environment,
- correct conditioning of your mind,
- having right thinking and attitudes, and by
- raising your effort-level.

The reason is simple –

"That is what you originally were and that is what **you can be now** again!"

9

The 5 S's and Human Needs

"Each human being lives always in domains of Five S's!"
One great Indian saint has once said –
   "A man (or woman) lives his (or her) life between Five S's – in domains of '5 S' always!"

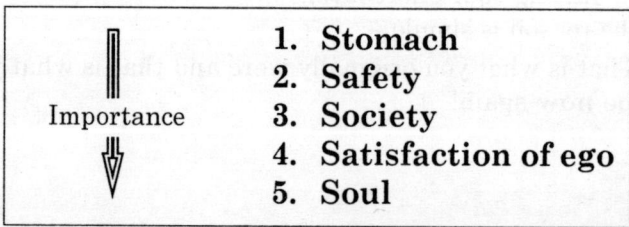

Most of the management books highlight the *hierarchy of human needs* as laid out by Abraham Maslow.

A striking correspondence may be observed here, between ancient Indian wisdom passed down the generations by words of mouth which is simplified by that great saint as *The 5 S's*, and the well-known *Hierarchy of Needs*.

However, the point of focus for you, here is – the relative levels of importance and evolution of human needs at each S-Domain or at each hierarchical level, and thus understand the difference people make to themselves and to others.

The 5 S's

1. Stomach
The first S-domain a person lives in is – stomach! It means that first a man, woman or a child always look for satisfying his or her hunger.

This is the reason why one works and does any activity. This urge assumes first priority for human beings and for animals both. Every living being requires food to live upon for physical growth. And all human beings as well as animals require food for functioning of their stomach.

2. Safety

The second S-domain a person lives-in is – safety.

It means once the stomach is full, a person looks for safety.

Safety is of two kinds.

The first-safety is from physical threats, from any harm. That is why one builds a house and lives in groups, villages and cities, so that one is safe and is away from any danger to one's life.

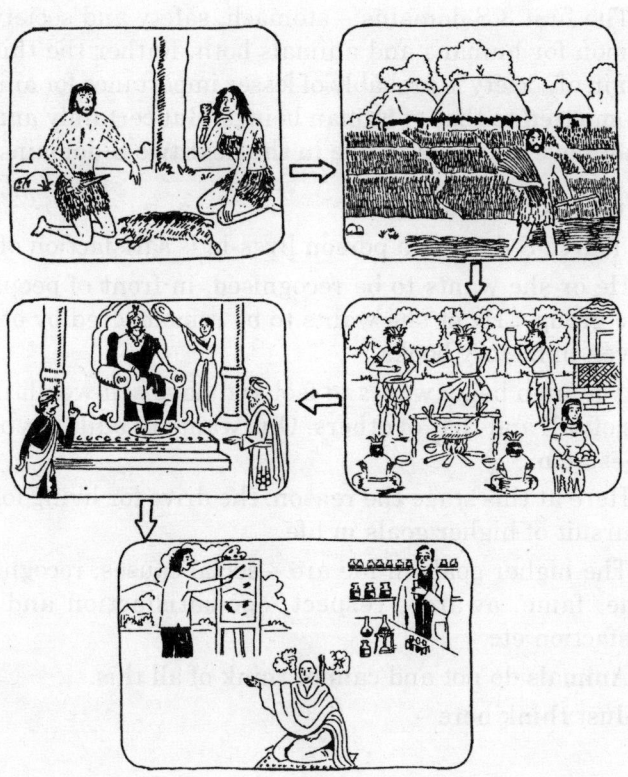

The second safety is of one's food. Safety of one's provisions to keep filling the stomach. That is why one stocks food. That is why a man or a woman look for a secure job. One works to ensure continuance of one's supply of food.

This S-domain of safety is common to human beings and animals – both live in houses and both stock food.

3. Society

The third S-domain a person lives in is – society. It means after filling the stomach and ensuring safety, one looks for society. Everyone wants to be loved.

Everyone wants to be appreciated. Everyone wants to share emotions. Human beings and animals both want expression of emotions. That is the reason one lives in groups. A person wants company and society.

The first 3 S-domains – stomach, safety and society are common for humans and animals both. Rather the third S-domain of society is probably of lesser importance for animals as compared to that of human beings. But certainly animals do not have potential to live in the next two S-domains.

4. Satisfaction of Ego

The fourth S-domain a person lives-in is satisfaction of ego.

He or she wants to be recognised, in front of people, in large groups. He or she wants to be remembered by others, or even in history books.

A human being wants to feel and have self-worth-in the eyes of self and that of others. One wants to build his or her self-esteem.

Here at this stage the reason, the drive for living for one is-pursuit of higher goals in life.

The higher goals in life are – social causes, recognition, name, fame, awards, respect, ego-satisfaction and self-satisfaction etc.

Animals do not and cannot think of all this.

Just think here –

"Human beings do think, do want, and do aspire for all this. But how many of us do this with sincerity and commitment.

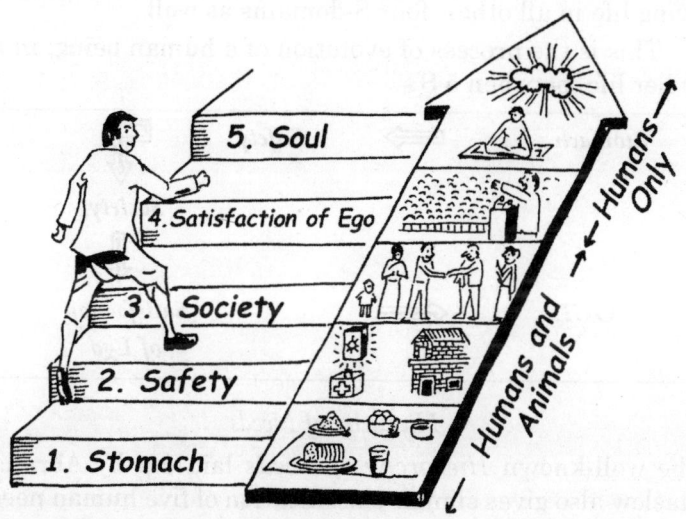

5. Soul

Finally, the fifth S-domain a person lives in is soul.

When one rises in life above the domains of stomach, safety, society, and satisfaction of ego – one looks for satisfying the needs of one's soul.

One manifests it in the form of 'creativity'.

All creations of human heart and mind flow from the life in this domain.

All immortal, invaluable, everlasting music, paintings, arts, handicrafts, monuments, sculptures, acts and performances, medicines, marvels of engineering and technology, architectures, inventions, discoveries, new theories and ideas etc. These all are creations of humans who live in the domain of soul, after rising above all other realms of their lives.

One also starts wondering, appreciating and understanding then the 'Creator' behind all 'creations', especially God-believers.

One searches for and lives for the goal of self-realisation.

Here one lives life mainly for his or her greater self for the domains of his or her soul – the higher self, while also living life in all other four S-domains as well.

This is the process of evolution of a human being, in his or her life, between 5 S's.

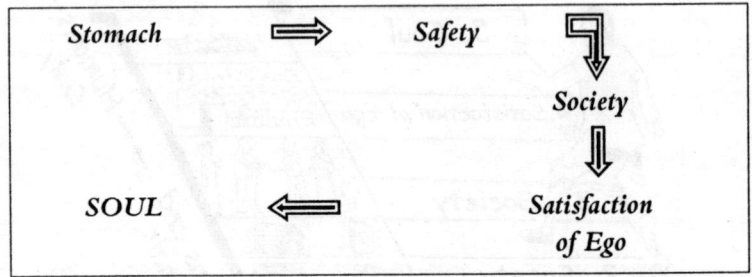

Hierarchy of Needs

The well-known *Hierarchy of Needs* laid out by Abraham Maslow also gives similar classification of five human needs.

It may be observed here also that *only after satisfying one's lower hierarchy need, a human being looks forward to the satisfaction of next need in higher order of hierarchy.*

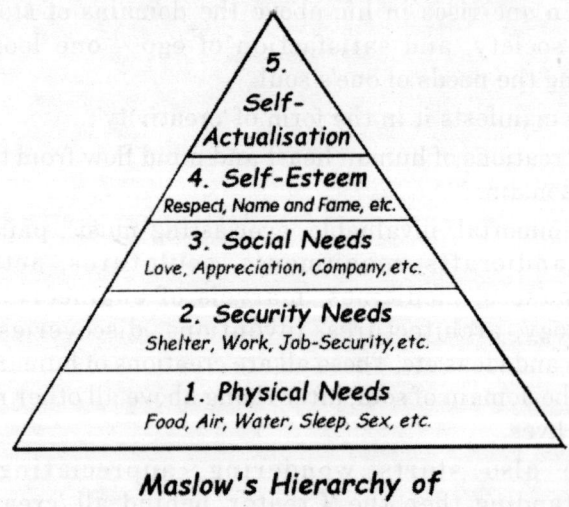

Maslow's Hierarchy of Five Human Needs

In modern times also, relevance of both of these concepts – of 5 domains and of human needs can be seen in one's day-to-day life. It is easy to find people who are living in any of the five domains of life to satisfy any of the 5 needs.

Correspondence of 5 S's and Human Needs

1. Stomach and physical needs

Many people live in the first-domain itself – stomach – the physical needs. Majority of population in the world just live for food and always remain in that world only.

It may be at times due to poverty, but still many well-to-do people also live only for enjoying good food.

People propagate philosophy – *'Eat, Drink and Be Merry!'* – in which the first two parts are pertaining mainly to stomach domain only.

Majority of the population is living life for stomach, sex and sleep – physical needs only.

2. Safety and security needs

Next, a little lesser population lives in the safety domain – for security needs.

The idea of having a house, or a shelter is manifestation of it. Poor think of a small house, and better-offs think of bigger luxurious houses for safety of themselves and of their nears and dears.

People also look for job security – for security of inflow of money and for security of their comforts.

That is why one does any work also.

Maintaining food-stocks are also results of this security need only.

3. Society and social-needs

Third comes **society** – domain – **social needs.** The majority of Indian population, rich, poor, and middle class all live in this domain for most of the periods of their long, but small lives.

Status – this is one word for which all these people keep running throughout their lives.

This hunger for appreciation by society is what, that drives one to seek various assets, accumulations like – bike, car, land, house, jewellery, bank-balance etc., and many other such status symbols.

All possessions of show-value, which may be considered adding to one's status, are focal points in the lives of people living in this domain.

Also the 'be merry' part of the philosophy *'Eat, Drink, and Be Merry'* – is what rules some people here. Entertainment visits to clubs, hotels, disco-theatres etc. all the ingredients of glamorous life, pomp and show; and fun, tourism and travel with family and friends, partying, various social functions and get-togethers etc. all the things representing and requiring appreciation, companionship and love-are part of one's social-needs only.

4. Satisfaction of ego and self-esteem needs

A smaller population lives-in and lives for the life of this fourth-level domain-self-esteem. These people in India and world both form a very small section of the population.

These people live for the sake of social causes-charity, helping others, some national or international issues etc.

They have a sincere urge of doing something for others, for society, for their motherland, and for the mankind as a whole.

They have compassion, sympathy, kindness, generosity, and belongingness to their roots-to people of their community, village, city, state, and country or of whole world.

The driving factors here may be-recognition, respect of others, name, fame, feeling of self-worth, satisfaction of ego, self-satisfaction or self-esteem etc.

These people can really be called big-people or big shots who make a difference to their own life and to lives of many others.

5. Soul and self-actualisation needs

Comprising the smallest of population of whole world living in this domain looks forward to creations of heart and mind.

They tend to take more of an internal journey pertaining to their soul-the self-the quest of their higher self. It has also been termed as self-actualisation – the search of truth.

Various inventions, discoveries and creations – all are outcomes as by-products of this internal quest.

All eminent and great people are born and made in the process of pursuits of this domain only.

These people are all great saints, teachers, philosophers, guides, preachers, leaders, social-workers, patriots, scientists, artists, doctors, lawyers, engineers, industrialists, businessmen, politicians, musicians, painters, architects, sculptors, farmers, craftsmen, poets, literary figures, performers and actors etc.

These people from all walks of life who, in their life *rise above a threshold level of excellence* in either fields of heart or mind, and all those also *who attain some significance in life that may be termed as eminence or greatness in real sense*, live in this domain predominantly.

The question you must ask to yourself!

The question, which *you* must ask to yourself now is-

"Which life you are living?"

or

"Which domain of life you are in?"

or

"Are you evolving?"

If your answer is yes then –

"From which domain to which domain you are evolving?"

A man or a woman lives life between either of '5 Ss'.

What makes a difference for one is –

"In which 'S-Domain' one is living and is spending his or her life?"

-Is it the lowest 'S' or the highest 'S'?

And that is what makes the whole difference to you, to your life and to all those others around you.

10

Five Healths and a Balanced Life!

"Life too needs 'a balance' like any other thing on earth!"

A balanced life!

To lead a balanced and successful life, a man or a woman requires good health in five areas. Or it may be said that one needs to live a balanced life, not lop-sided.

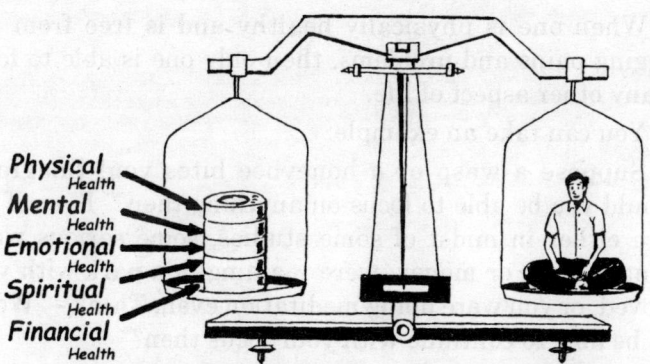

And that is possible, only when one is enjoying all the five kinds of healths – physical, mental, emotional, spiritual and financial.

Five healths

One can be called healthy only if one is healthy in all these five aspects of life or maintains good status of all the following five healths:-

    1. Physical health

2. Mental health
3. Emotional health
4. Spiritual health
5. Financial health

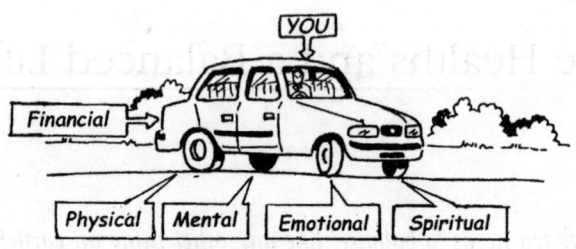

You and Your Vehicle of Life!

1. Physical health

It is of utmost importance. It has been said –

"A sound mind stays in a sound body!"

When one is physically healthy and is free from any nagging pains and problems, then only one is able to focus on any other aspect of life.

You can take an example: -

Suppose a wasp or a honeybee bites you! Imagine – "Would you be able to focus on anything then?" Even if you were either in midst of some studies, some serious work, counting cash or money, were roaming in a park with your beloved, or you were doing meditation even. Think – "Would you be able to continue with your focus then?"

No, certainly not.

You will surely be disturbed for sometime, till that pain subsides, or you will control that pain either by some medicine or by curing it mentally. That is why it has been said in India – "You cannot even worship God if you are hungry!" Therefore, you definitely need to have good physical health.

In this age of pollution (air, water, noise, mental and environmental pollution) and adulteration (in fruits, vegetables, all eatables, milk, ghee, oil etc.), maintaining good physical health and staying free from any disease is a real boon for one.

You also need to be cautious in your eating habits, for-

"Less diseases and deaths have occurred due to eating less, than more diseases and deaths have taken place due to eating more!"

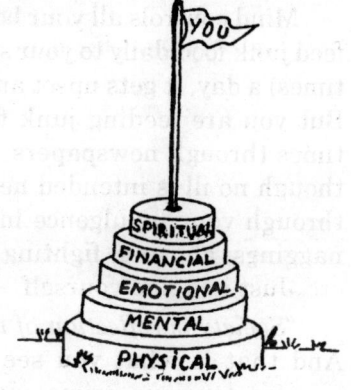

Few suggestions to maintain good physical health
(As told by age-old Indian wisdom and by modern doctors too.)
- Eat moderately.
- Change contents of eatables you take – to more of fruits and vegetables. Have less of fats and more of vitamins and energetic things.
- Have regularity in eating and sleeping. Eat and sleep at regular time, in regular quantity.
- Exercise daily. Do some physical exercise, yoga asanas, sports-activities, walking or jogging. Whatever exercise is convenient to you and in howsoever less or more duration you may be able to do exercise, but doing it on a daily basis is essential for good physical health.
- Have fresh air for some time daily.
- Smile and laugh daily.

2. *Mental health*

Physical health is important, very important but not the only thing important in life. To stay healthy one needs all kinds of other healths also – more so the mental health. It is also linked to one's IQ – intelligence quotient.

It has already been discussed and illustrated in this book – "you feed to your stomach daily but what do you feed to your mind?"

Mind controls all your bodily chores and functions. If you feed junk food daily to your stomach at all meals (two or three times) a day, it gets upset and you land up in bed or hospital! But you are feeding junk food daily to your mind, all the times through newspapers, magazines, TV and movies etc., though no ill is intended here against these industries; and through your indulgence in gossips, criticisms, complaints, naggings, abusing, fighting over trivia, cribbing and crying etc. Just imagine yourself – "where would you land up?"

"Society is reflection of mankind" – is an old-age saying. And that is what you see around and you get-miseries, worries, tensions, crime, violence and corruption.

Throughout the day and throughout your life – "when do you actually feed any good mental food to your mind?" Your mind also needs some good mental food sometimes. It is therefore a necessity for you, to correct your thinking and your attitudes, if you care for your mental health.

There is also a saying –

"Empty mind is devil's workshop!" So, keep your mind busy.

If you do not use your brain, it gets rusted.

Yes, your mind also is like a machine, like a vehicle. If you leave it unused and unattended for some time, it deteriorates faster.

Five Healths and a Balanced Life! ■ 99

Just try to recollect anything which you had read some 10-15 years back and you have not used, applied or required that knowledge till date. For example geography – say length, width, area of India, or say latitudes and longitudes of the city you are in right now (tell without GPS-Global Positioning System). Can you recollect it now?

– Chances are, you may not recollect it now, since you might not have used this information for a long time.

Therefore use your mind, feed it daily.

Few suggestions to maintain good mental health

- Read some good books on a daily basis. Read something that is good, uplifting, knowledge-giving, mind-churning, thought-provoking and which evolves you. But what's important is that you must read it daily for some time, preferably before sleep at night or after waking up in the morning.
- Develop habit of writing anything regularly or involve yourself in any mental work, which forces you to think and stretch your mental muscles.
- Listen to good talks or lectures through audio or videotapes, or CDs of successful, motivating and elevated people.
- Attend seminars, lectures, conventions etc., of uplifting and motivating nature.
- Associate yourself with successful, good and motivated people having positive attitudes and self-confidence. Make friendships and healthy relationships with them. Interact with them frequently, may be even on a daily basis.
- Reduce negative inputs to your mind to as small quantity as you can.
- Check all inputs before it enters your mind, for mental viruses.

- Always remember – *"Only light can dispel darkness!"*

Light dispels Darkness!

3. Emotional health

You do need emotional health too. In this modern age one needs good EQ – Emotional Quotient also, for a balanced life and success.

Human beings live with and do carry a wide variety of emotions and other attributes – pleasure, anger, fear, love, hate, irritation, despair, hope, boldness, courage, cowardice, adventurism, compassion, pity, sympathy etc. All these need proper handling.

It has been told by all Indian saints and has also been proved by modern age scientists and doctors that uncontrolled and suppressed emotions cause various troubles and disorders – mental and physical both.

Mental disorders, diseases, psychological troubles and even many physical ailments as various psychosomatic diseases etc., are the result of improper handling of various human emotions. Lack of good emotional health also gives birth to alcoholism, drug-addiction, frustration and even crime, suicides and insecure environment.

Whereas good emotional health provides you on one hand a proper environment of love, cooperation, support, good community living, helping others, team spirit and mutually-uplifting gestures etc. On the other hand even the emotions like pleasure, love, joy, happiness and satisfaction are also enhanced among individuals by good emotional health.

Like your mind you need to feed your heart too (for emotions), though it is a functional part of brain only.

Few suggestions to have good emotional health

- Develop positive, uplifting attitudes and feelings in you, even by mere imaginations at times.
- Create, find, nurture and nourish your dream in life. Never ever suppress it. Be sincere to it and also be ready to work for it.
- Have some emotional outlet necessarily. Never suppress any emotion by harsh methods. If at all any negative emotions you have, attenuate those by more of positive thinking. Or you may share those emotions by way of talking, writing or speaking with someone close, confident and positive-minded person.
- Release your emotions through some worthy outlet. Write those out, tell or speak those out to somebody who is close to you and is a positive person. Best would be to express your emotions through some creations like poetry, writing articles or essays, drawing, singing, speaking, helping others etc. Or you may also utilise your emotions as catalysts for your own determination further towards some worthy cause, some artistic creation, some invention, discovery or for some adventure etc.
- Listen to good music – soft, soothing, slow, and uplifting – at those times when you have moments of excessive emotions.
- Develop good friendships in every city you visit. Talk to people, observe, and share. Go for tourism, travel and sightseeing with family and friends occasionally.

- Keep yourself more in good, positive, healthy environment for more time. See sunrise daily. Do it as far as possible. Love nature.
- Follow the age-old wisdom –

"Replace hate with love, critics with appreciation, complaints and problems with solutions and anger with compassion".

All these steps and good emotions will be beneficial to you only. It is very much required for your emotional health and a balanced life.

4. Spiritual health

Just look at a light bulb.
- What gives light in it? Is this the glass of bulb, or the tungsten element of it or is it something else?

   Look at a fresh rose bud in the morning.
- What makes it grow?

   Look at a dead body and yourself.

– What is the difference?
Answer to all these questions is –

> **Life
> The Vital Force!**

Good spiritual health is that which provides you energy, wisdom-beliefs, attitudes, will and then pleasure, happiness and satisfaction in life.

"It is the fountainhead of life, which keeps one's all other healths also intact."

You might have felt, experienced or might have heard people talking of vanity in life, purposelessness, lack of direction, lack of meaning in life or worthlessness.

It is all due to lack of spiritual health or due to spiritual imbalance.

Spiritual health provides some meaning, some direction, worth, fulfilment, self-respect, self-esteem, drive, energy and motivation to do something creative and constructive in life. It also gives one some focus, a purpose and a perspective in life.

Few suggestions to attain good spiritual health

(As, preached by ancient Indian saints, Vedas and by world's spiritual leaders)

- Believing in God (for believers), in whatever 'name' and 'form' you believe in, is the best way to attain good spiritual health. You just have to nurture it on a routine basis and you need to strengthen your faith daily.
- Even if you are an atheist, you too can have ways –
  Belief in yourself, or belief in some super-consciousness or in some cosmic-consciousness, or at least belief in your own conscience, upholding your conscience at all times and following your own inner voice are few of the best ways of attaining good spiritual health.

- Do meditation daily at morning and preferably at evening too. Duration of meditation can be varying from 5 minutes to 30 minutes for each sitting.
- Mantra-*japa*, *naam-japa*, *yajana*, performing Vedic rituals, recital of Vedic-shlokas or remembering and praying the name, form or shape in which you believe in God – are other suggested means of attaining good spiritual health.

5. Financial health

When one talks of blood one talks of heart. But what about *veins*, which facilitate the flow of blood?

When one talks of books one thinks of papers and pen but *ink* is that which makes it all possible.

You may think of car, driver, skills etc. But fuel is that which makes it run.

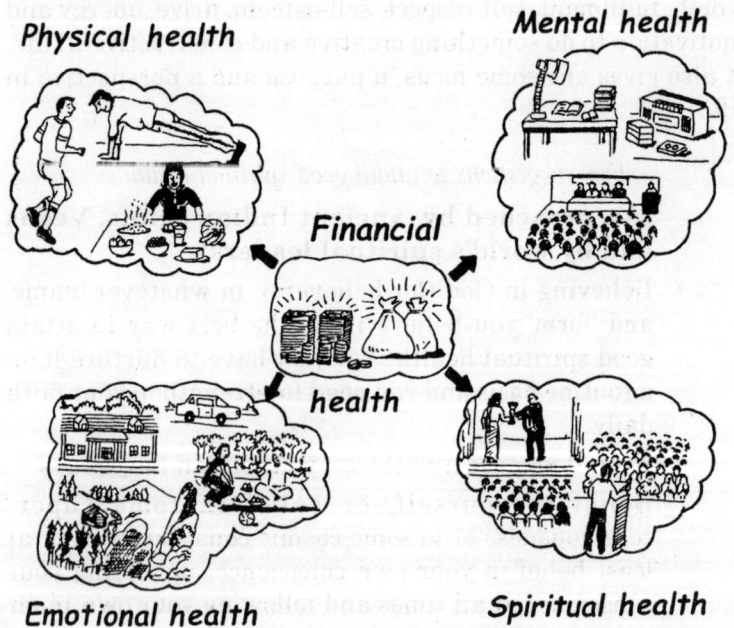

Likewise, money, finance, your financial health is that blood, that ink, that fuel, which facilitates all your other four healths.

Someone has said – "It is not important how much money you make, but important is, what you do with that money?"

- "Money is not an end in itself, but money is means to an end!"
- "Money is a tool-a really powerful tool – but how you use it, is up to you!"
- "Money is not everything. But it provides options in life.

Good food for physical health costs money. Good books, tapes and seminars for mental health will cost money! Entertainment, fun, music, adventure, sightseeing, travel and tourism, partying, social exchanges and obligations – necessary for emotional health will also require finance. Good, comfortable, luxurious life too needs good financial health! Even charity, helping others and many spiritual pursuits too need finance.

"Good financial health enhances the area of your reach and effectiveness greatly."

And why you should not have it? When you are competent, capable, deserving, and a worthy person, then why should you be living a life of deprivation?

Financial health with other four healths would provide you a complete, satisfying and a fulfilled life.

The only caution is that in pursuit of financial health you have to guard yourself and must stay away from vices, lust, greed and pseudo-pride. Else, your all other four healths would also deteriorate.

Suggestions for achieving good, stable and long-term financial-health are made in the next chapter.

"All five healths – physical, mental, emotional, spiritual and financial health, thus give you a balance in life."

It is then that you would get true pleasure, meaning in life, worth, purpose, happiness and satisfaction.

Truly speaking, a good status of other four healths would act as counter-balance to the fifth – your spiritual health.

"All these five healths are like five balloons of different colours. It would be challenging for you to hold all of the five balloons together at a time, but you also cannot afford to ignore and leave any one balloon of health!"

You have to get it all, and you must get it.

There is also a striking correspondence and similarity between the five S's and five healths.

- Both can be obtained.
- Both are important.

Remember always:

> It's your life!
> and
> you must live it fully!

11

Four Ways of Making Money and Education

There is a difference between earning money and making money, but for discussion sake both are referred here by either of the single term making money or earning money.

Money in itself may not be all that important in one's life and in one's priority order, but still it is quite important for one.

There are four ways of making money.

All occupations, professions, and all works people do or function as, to get their livelihood, can be categorised into the following four:

1. Job or service employees

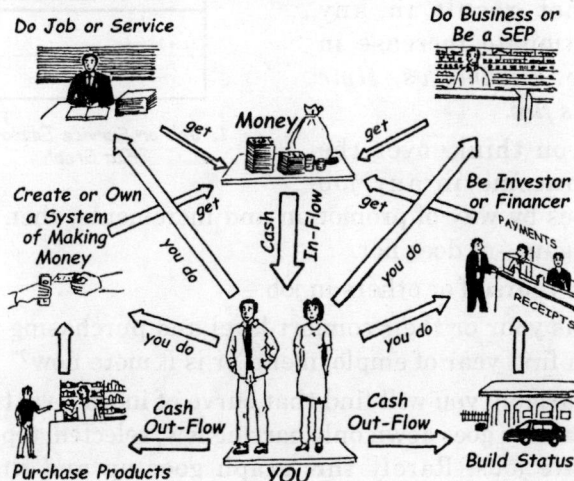

2. Business owners or self-employed professionals (SEPs)
3. System creators or system owners
4. Investors or financers

Four financial categories

Category 1
Job or service employees

Majority of population in the world earns livelihood by doing some job or service. As a job-employee by working for somebody else or for some organisation, no one really makes money – one only earns a salary for his or her services.

Still people pick up a job-employment, because majority, particularly in India, consider a job to be safe and secure.

Just think –

"Are jobs really safe and secure?"

If you plot a graph of income vs. time (put in job) for people working as employee in any job or service, it is a flat-graph.

Any amount of hours may be put, in a job or service on daily basis, but it does not result in any proportionate increase in income. *Income vs. time graph is flat.*

1. Job or Service Employees
Flat Graph

If you think, over the years income in any job increases by way of promotion and increments, then check it out again – it does not.

Ask yourself or others in job –

"Was your or their comfort level and purchasing power more in first year of employment, or is it more now?"

Invariably you will find that curve of income vs. time in a job actually goes down only barring few, selected, top-notch corporate jobs. Rarely this graph goes up and that too marginally only-else by and large it remains flat. The salary level may increase but not really the income.

It is almost the same scenario of every employee – whether one is in any government service or is in any private, public sector or multinational corporate job.

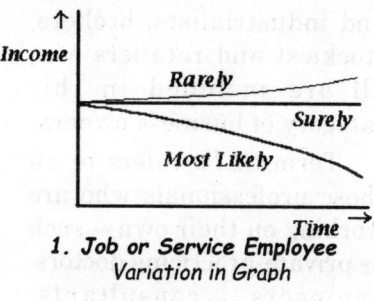
1. Job or Service Employee Variation in Graph

There exists nothing like a dream job. No such thing exists in real life. It is merely an illusion. Someone has said it well "Person who has dreams works for himself, and who does not works for others."

It is a very widely spread and deep-rooted myth in all societies and all nations across the globe, that – "Pick-up a job, and you get everything in life as well as security of life as an employee."

But no, it is not so. It is not the reality.

JOB is 'Just Over Broke' – and it is true for most of the people in a job or service. Intention here is not to condemn doing jobs, but it is to rather discuss the dynamics of it and remove the illusions most people have regarding jobs.

What a price it is to pay for this kind of pseudo-job security.

Fear of boss or losing one's job is the motivation here, which alone works for every job or service employee, most of the time. And which is a very low-level motivational factor because it is negative motivation.

Category 2
Business owners or self-employed professionals (SEPs)

Another majority of population worldwide earns livelihood by either being in some kind of business or by being a self-employed professional as defined in chapter two.

Traders, farmers, shop-keepers, vendors, contractors, showroom-owners, cottage-small-middle level manufactures and industrialists, brokers, stockiest and retailers etc., all are included in this category of business owners.

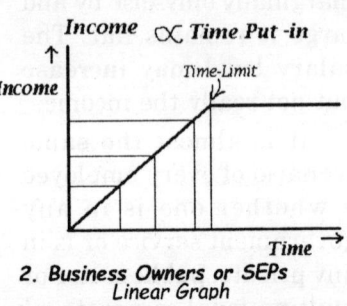

2. Business Owners or SEPs Linear Graph

Term *SEPs* refers to all those professionals who are working on their own – such as private-practicing doctors, engineers, consultants, lawyers, architects, detectives, chartered accountants, freelance journalists, professional players, professional artists and performers etc.

All these people in this category have one thing in common – their income-level increases in direct proportion to number of hours they put-in.

Income is linearly proportional to time.

It means-if these people work for, say 4 hours a day, they earn some money. Now if they put-in 8 hours a day, then their income-level is doubled.... and so on. It also means- the day they do not work, they earn nothing! And that is the big trap.

People in this category have advantage of being their own boss. But the disadvantage is that in these kinds of business people apparently own; the fact is-their business owns them. They seldom get time to enjoy their money with their family because fear of financial loss is the motivation here, which also is negative motivation.

Moreover these people also have a limitation – a ceiling on their income level, since physically and humanly it is not possible to work for an infinite period of time daily. "How many hours a day one can put in his or her work?" – 15, 20 or 24 hours a day. Not more as that is the *limitation* here.

Category 3
System creators or system owners

These are the people who create a system or own the system. Generally known as big shots – these people are the owners of big-business houses or business groups.

Their income vs. time graph is exponential.

They get multiplicative income.

These people create a system, say by putting-in few million rupees or so, in some project — may be opening a factory etc. Then they institutionalise it and create a system. They hire people from Category-1 as their employees-as workers may be skilled or unskilled, supervisors, managers, and engineers or may be as financial, legal, administrative expert etc. All those people who do job or service for them and get regular salary, are their employees.

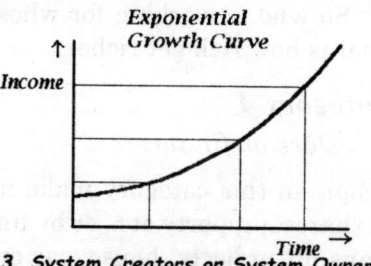

3. **System Creators or System Owners**
Exponential Curve

They hire people or get them from Category-2 as stockiest, retailers, agents or brokers etc., who all work on the system created and owned by these people of this category.

Over a period of time this system created by them multiplies exponentially in terms of turnover, net-worth, size and yielding income. It grows from that few million rupees to worth tens, hundreds or thousands of millions of rupees and more.

Think – "Does salary of their employees from Category 1 doing job for them, increase in the same proportion?" – no!

"Does profit or commission earned by Category 2 people working on the system of these people increase in same proportion?"-no!

Also think, "Who works on the system?"

"Do these people, system creator or owner of it work themselves more on their system?"

Or other people in Category 1 or 2 work more on their system and multiply their wealth?

So who is working for whose dreams? Decide yourself. That is how rich get richer.

Category 4
Investors or financers

People in this category make money by either investing it in shares, property etc., or by financing others – giving them loans for projects, house, car or for other household things etc.

You must have heard and must have known that people make big money by investing or by financing, but a constraint here is that they need good amount of seed money to start with.

But, after that –

"How do these people make money?"

– They use principle of leveraging – By using time-

Leveraging

leverage and money-leverage, like conventional *lever*. By using a lever-even with 10 kg force you can lift weight of even 50 kg.

Likewise it is possible by money-leveraging that you invest one million rupees and take returns of 3, 5 or 10

Four Ways of Making Money and Education ▪ 113

millions out of it. Where as in conventional business that most people do in Category 2, one invests 10 million rupees and returns are mere 1 or 2 million rupees only.

Similarly, it is also possible by time-leveraging that you invest one-hour efforts, and take returns equal to 10, 100 hours of effort or more.

These people in this Category 4 also get exponential income – their income vs. time graph is also exponential.

However, people in Category 3 or 4 do take more risks also, apart from having good investment capital, that is how they make money.

Few observations

Observe a few things now, related to money and financial world.

Observation 1

The 80:20 division of wealth

"How many people in the world are in Category 1 or 2?"

In other words – "How many people are doing either job, service, business or are self-employed?"

– At least 80 per cent!

"How many people in the world are in category 3 or 4?", which means – "How many people in the world are either system-creators or system owners? Or how many are investors or financers?"

– Not more than 20 per cent!

Observe now –

"Where is the wealth of the world?" Who holds the money? Who rules the roost?

– At least 80 per cent of total wealth of the world is with people in category 3 or 4, and not more than 20 per cent of it is with people in category 1 or 2.

Observation 2
Myth of academics and degrees

It is a widespread myth, particularly in India, that – "A person who gets more academic qualifications, a person who acquires more degrees can earn more money."

Many people believe in it. People, especially if they are not earning sufficient money and belong either to poor villages or to middle-class, blame it to non-pursuance of their academics – their school or college education.

People continue to acquire and urge getting more and more stamps on them, in the form of various degrees and certificates, just under the belief that it would fetch them more money.

This nation is a big farce.

Observe now that –"Which category of people have more academics – more degrees?"

You will find that people of Category 1 or 2 have even highest academic qualifications and more academics in

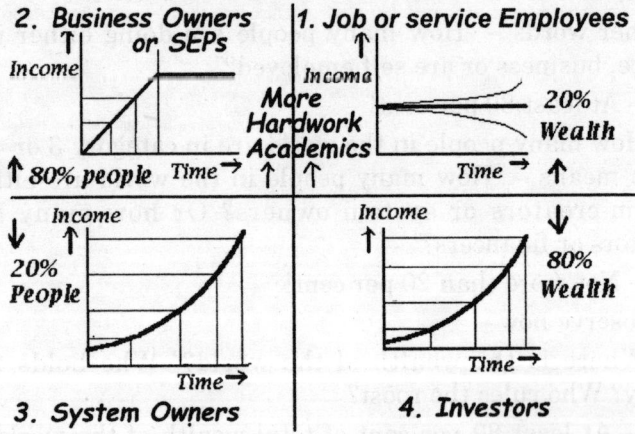

general. Whereas people in Category 3 or 4 may be illiterate also.

Also, "If only academic qualification was to fetch all the wealth, then all school teachers and college professors should have been the richest, or should have been among the wealthy people at least!

Observation 3

Myth of hard work

Another widespread myth is –

"A person who does more hard work earns more or makes more money!"

And surprisingly, believing it people continue to slog more and more in life.

Observe – "Which category of people do more hardwork?"

You will find that people in Category 1 or 2 do more slogging daily – early morning to late nights even, whereas people in Category 3 or 4, may hardly be working for few hours.

Also "If only hardwork was the criterion for making wealth, then a labourer should have been the richest in the world, and all labourers wealthy. However, this is certainly not true.

Faulty programming
regarding academics and money

Though there are four ways of earning or making money but what have you been programmed for? – "What have you been told and taught, right from your childhood?"

Do well in academics, get good grades, more degrees and eventually good job. That will be the gateway to your success and you will get everything in life."

Or – "Get good academics. Do some business. Be a professional. Be self-employed. And you will be successful as well as wealthy then!"

Right from your childhood, that is what you have been told and taught by parents, brothers, sisters, friends, relatives, neighbours, school-teachers, college professors and by everybody else. That is what you have been programmed for.

Even today, in India, if you are asked as a parent that – "What do you want your children to be in life? What would you tell them to aspire for and become in life?"

Invariably your choices would be like "an engineer, a doctor, a lawyer, an MBA, a chartered accountant, a civil servant or a businessman etc."

Observe – "Where would one land up then?"

– In Category 1 or 2!

Introspect – "Have you ever been told till date, how you can get in Category 3 or 4 (if you are not there already)?"

– Perhaps no! You have only been taught and told – how to get to Category 1 or 2.

And that is the faulty programming done to you, regarding academics and money.

What do you want in life?

Just reflect back in your life and recollect –"What you wanted or still want to have, to do and to be?"

- Own a house or may be a bungalow;
- Own a cycle, a scooter, a motorbike, a car or a bigger car;
- Entertainment, enjoyment, fun or travel and tours with family and friends;
- Do charity;
- Be wealthy;
- Helping others;
- Give good education to children;
- Become a legend in life;
- Get name, fame etc.

Think – "Where – in which category does this list get fulfilled?"

"Is it in category 1?" No, it does not.

"Is it in category 2?" Partly!

"Where fully then?" In Category 3 or 4!

Does that mean – "You would like to migrate from category 1 or 2 to category 3 or 4."

But you must think – "What is the vehicle with you? Do you have millions of rupees to invest in?" – No.

Four Ways of Making Money and Education ▪ 117

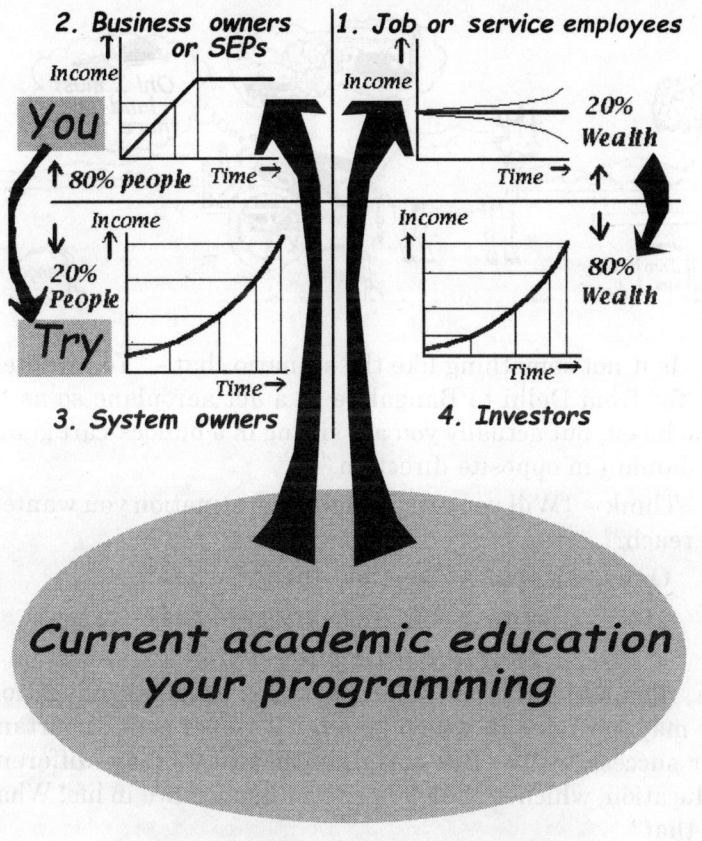

Then – "what is going to be your vehicle?"

You will say – academics, academic education or more degrees.

But – "where will it lead to?"

To category 1 or 2 only.

Oh! This is surely a mismatch.

See the opposing direction of arrows in the picture shown on the facing page. See the contrast – "Where you wanted to go, where you are going and where would you land up?"

Wake-Up Call in the Wee Hours

Is it not something like the scenario that – "You wanted to 'fly' from Delhi to Bangalore in a Jet aeroplane so as to reach fast, but actually you are sitting in a bullock-cart going to Jammu in opposite direction."

Think – "Will you ever reach the destination you wanted to reach?"

Or even if you say 'yes', but then – "when?"

How rich and successful Be rich and successful?

Rich and successful may have this academic education or may not have it, which is only 10-15 per cent important for success in life. But certainly they have some different education, which is of 85-90 per cent importance in life! What is that?

Let us list it out:
- *Communication skills* – How to talk to others?
- *People skills* – How to connect with people?
- *Handling people* – How to handle various people of varying types and temperaments?
- *Tact* – Where and how to get the work done?
- *Goal setting and strategies* – to achieve goals!
- *Team building* – How to build, nurture, maintain and develop a winning-team?
- *Leadership* – How to lead people to deliver the best in them, for their goals?
- *Vision*-Seeing what others do not see yet!
- *Developing Leaders* – How to develop others into able leaders?

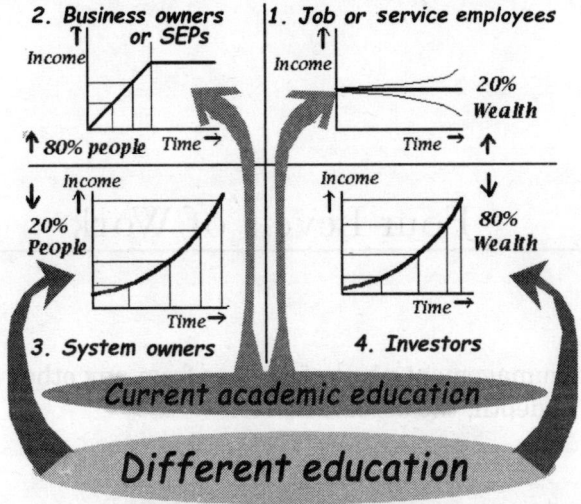

The Real Education

Introspect here – "Aren't these, all listed above, the parameters of success in life? Are these not required in any walk of life-in job, business or self-employment – to be successful?"

That is the education the real education which our schools and colleges do not provide, which rich pass to their children and to heirs only, to none else!

This is the real education of 85-90 per cent importance in life, which you need for yourself even and need to pass it on to your children.

12

Four Levels of Work

From management point of view or from any other angle, if seen in depth, the observation is:

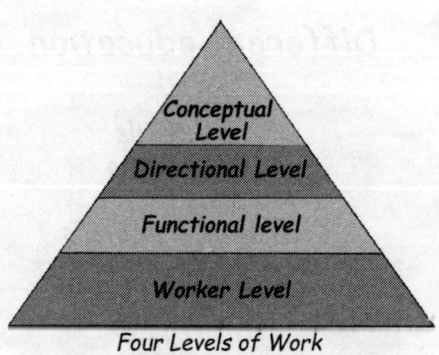

Four Levels of Work

*"A man or a woman always works at either of above **four-levels** in his or her life-in any organisation, in any field or in any walk of life!"*

Four levels of work

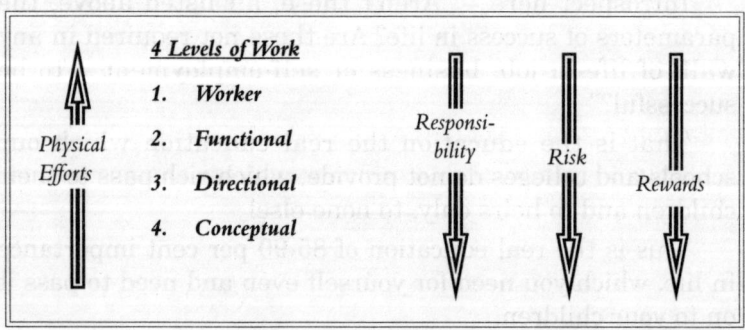

1. Worker level
Shop-floor level or grassroot level

In an organisation's hierarchy, this is the bottom level, which forms base of the organisation's pyramid.

In the pyramid shown above, the width of each horizontal bar also indicates population at that level. The term population here indicates the percentage of aggregate population of that organisation's structure.

Various responsibilities, authority, area of exercising these and corresponding rewards in terms of income, luxuries, perks and privileges are also the least at this level.

2. Functional level
Supervisor level or junior-managerial level

A person at this level has to deal more with grassroot workers most of the time, while acting as interface between workers and management.

With increased domain of responsibility and authority, one gets more privileges and rewards at this level as compared to those at worker level.

But population at this level is certainly less than that at worker level. A ratio between supervisors to worker level varies from 1:3 to 1:20, with the ideal ratio being 1:3 and average ratio 1:10, depending on various factors.

3. Directional level
Middle level or senior management level

One rises to considerably higher positions in an organisation's hierarchy, at this level. Here a person deals more with top-management, owners or conceptual-level people, while taking assistance from and providing support, help and guidance to functional level personnel.

As indicated in the pyramid structure shown earlier, population of the aggregate is very less here. The ratio between directional level to functional-level population varies from 1:3 to 1:10, with 1:5 being the average ratio. Several intermediate layers may also exist here, or may be created if it is a larger organisation.

4. Conceptual level
Top-leadership level or owner level

"One is like the captain of a ship, or like the pilot of a passenger aircraft here."

One can rock the boat, with everybody on-board sinking together, or one may sail it successfully with all passengers safe and sound.

One may also fly the aeroplane successfully even in bad weathers, while facilitating everybody on-board to reach their destinations safely.

Risk factors, costs of failure and challenges are highest at this level, considering the domain of one's responsibility and authority as well. Therefore rewards and privileges are also biggest at this level.

However utmost transparency, confidence and faith of all lower level personnel is required to be achieved, by the people at this level.

Total population of the aggregate population of an organisation is least here it may even be countable at fingertips.

There may be several layers additionally created at each level, in case of bigger organisations. Most of the times, it is restricted to a maximum of 10 such layers and levels.

From worker level to conceptual level the risk factors, challenge, costs of failure and other stakes rise sharply, and so are the gains, rewards, perks and privileges etc. Risks and rewards always have a proportional relationship.

NO RISK, NO GAIN!
AS MUCH RISK, AS MUCH GAIN!

Requirement of various skills and knowledge at four-levels of work

Let us see now, what are the various skills and knowledge requirement, at each of these broad four levels of work.

All skills and knowledge required at various levels can be divided in two broad categories:

1. Technical or domain-specific skills

It encompasses all skills, knowledge and expertise required for a specific job, a specific domain of activity, or a specific role. It means, here one needs a domain-specific skill, expertise or knowledge.

Example: A doctor's medical knowledge, an engineer's technical skills, an accountant's financial knowledge, an administrator's administrative skills, a worker's expertise over his job or an artist's adeptness at his performance etc., are the examples of domain-specific skills.

2. General skills

Hereby the term general skills, reference is made to skills required by one, which are more of humane nature – are more people-oriented.

It encompasses skills like-communication skills, people skills, managerial skills and leadership quality etc.

It also encompasses the attributes like – tact, vision, initiative, confidence, courage, will-power, determination, goal-setting ability, strategic-thinking, potential to grasp a thing and situation, decision-making ability, ability of quicker and in depth assessment of situations, risks, stakes or of costs etc., – along with all other individual traits also like – analytical ability, assertiveness, persistence, patience and perseverance etc. All these skills and traits are coexistent as a result of one's thinking, beliefs, attitudes and level of efforts.

A Fact: A Startling Revelation

Assume you are heading a factory, a business of your own, which is your own organisation. Assume you have recently started it at a smaller scale.

Case 1: Transition from level 1 to level 2

Assume you have 10 workers at grassroot level. Your factory or that business is expanding and you need a supervisor now to manage these 10 people and to look after this part of your business.

"Whom will you appoint as a supervisor or a junior manager?"

To the person who has been your best performer at grassroot level, a person who has best technical skills? Or to the person who has excellent may not best technical skills, but who can manage other 10 workers, and can manage your business too – a person who has some general skills too.

Pause here. Think! You answer would be – "To second type person."

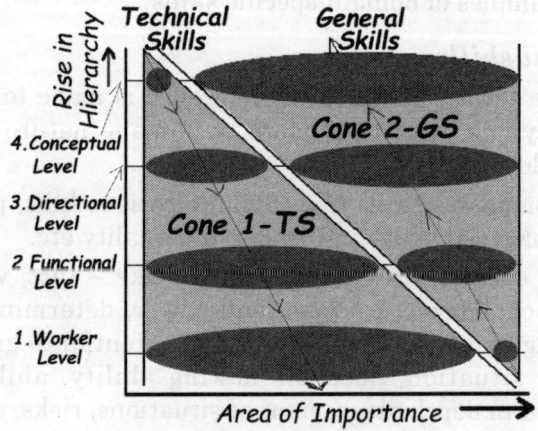

TS & GS Cones

Case 2: Transition from level 2 to level 3

Assume you have a workforce of 110 people now. You have 100 grass-root workers and 10 supervisors or junior managers. You want to expand your business to inter-city or inter-state level now by opening other branches. You need some senior managers now to look after your business in a city, a state or in a region, so that you may *focus* now on other cities, states or regions.

"Whom will you appoint as regional manager now?"

Four Levels of Work ■ 125

A person who has been the best at supervisor level! Or – the person who has good technical skills but who has very good general skills necessary to lead a team of 10 junior managers or supervisors.

If now again you say, "the second type person" then – "are you beginning to understand a chemistry of TS-GS cones?"

Case 3: Transition from level 3 to level 4

Assume you have 1110 personnel in your organisation now – 1000 workers, 100 supervisors or junior managers, and 10 senior managers or regional managers. You want to grow your organisation now at national or global level.

"Whom will you appoint as CEO or general manager of your company?"

Most probably you will say – "the person who has **best or excellent** general skills, and may be good or average technical skills."

The point to focus

The point to focus upon is obvious.

"Which cone is important for rise in life? Which cone is diminishing and which cone is expanding in area of importance?

Which cone is required more for your own growth or for any organisation's growth?"

> *Which 'cone' is more important for success' in life?*
> - *TS Cone – of technical skills? Or*
> - *GS Cone – of general skills?*

Ask yourself!
    Introspect!
        Think!
            Analyse now!!

> *Which 'cone' you have been focusing so far?*
> *-For your development*
> *and*
> *-For your growth*
> *TS Cone'?*
> *Or*
> *GS Cone'!!*

In all probability, you too must have been focusing so far on TS cone only – like so many others.

That is what majority does, particularly in India at least. People usually think –

"More education fetches more!"

The statement seems true.

But the question is –

"Which education fetches more?"

- One, which is in TS domain, or
- The one that pertains to GS Domain!"

Introspect –

> "Where
> is
> your
> focus?"

> **TAKE AIM!**
> **FOCUS CORRECTLY!!**

13

The Hidden Secrets!

"What you need to understand, are the secrets kept hidden from you in your journey of life so far!"

The truths untold

Truth 1: The 80-20 Rule

Researches world over in various fields bring out evidences of a truth that –

"80 per cent activities in life are often of 20 per cent importance only, whereas 20 per cent activities, often ignored, might be of 80 per cent importance!"

In the same way in any organisation "80 per cent people do only 20 per cent of the job, whereas 20 per cent people do 80 per cent job importance-wise."

In other words, the truth is – those "80 per cent accomplish only 20 per cent, whereas 20 per cent people accomplish four times more than those!"

The fact is, this training is often not imparted in any of the schools and colleges, except in very few business schools.

But you need to train yourself now to **focus** that:

> *What is yours that 20 per cent area of activities, of efforts or of your abilities, which you have been neglecting so far, which is of 80 per cent importance and which you must focus upon now?*

Truth 2: Education-The 10 per cent and 90 per cent

"Whatever we learn conventionally at schools and colleges – how much percentage of that education you would like to attribute to one's success in life?"

The fact remains that the old saying and oft-repeated words –"Education is important in one's life" – are absolutely true.

But the question is –

"Which education?"

"Which education is important? How much important this education is?"

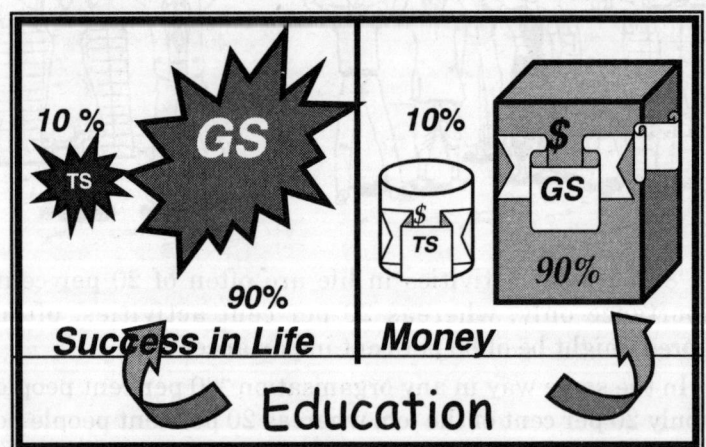

"Academic education is hardly of 10 per cent importance for success in one's life!"

It provides only a launching platform for a job or a career.

This is fine but focus now that, even in any job-interview – "what is the criterion of selection-obviously other than any push-pull or bribery?"

"Is it merely one's degrees and marks – the TS part of education?"

Or "How one presents himself or herself during the interview-the GS part of education" – that decides it?

And after that interview, in life or even in career, think – "what is going to fetch more? What is going to contribute more for success in life?"

You will find that –

"90 per cent contribution to success in your life would be of general skills – that other education, which is not imparted to you while pursuing your academics."

This 90 per cent important education is not given in any school, college or text books.

You have to find ways and means to equip yourself with this GS part of education – some of which is discussed in this book itself later.

Here, one thing must be made very clear.

The objective here is not at all to demean or belittle the academics part – the TS part of education, nor it is to condemn all those great institutions, schools and colleges. Rather the objective here is to bring out the limitations of this education system.

Objective here is to bring the focus upon a truth that –

"This current education-system all over the world, particularly in India, is geared-up only for churning out job-oriented people or professionals."

"It is merely focused at helping one to earn some livelihood or to improve one's income level a little bit only."

"This current education system does not help one to explore his or her full potential."

This current education system does not really facilitate one to explore, express or realise one's enormous potential, in the fields of heart or mind.

One's potential keeps just lying dormant most of the times and gradually goes down the drain, without actually benefitting either the individual or the world.

Truth 3: Need of Morals, Virtues and Other Positive Attributes

Many of you might have experienced in life that the words and attributes like – morals, virtues, honesty, integrity and sincerity etc. – seem to be gradually losing their importance and meaning in society, more so in the Indian context.

These words and attributes, which were once regarded must in all societies and countries, are doubted today about their efficacy and practicability in present times.

Questions are raised today, by so-called intellectuals and even by young minds that –

"Why do we need morals, virtues and other positive attributes in our lives? What do we gain by these?"

Concerns, doubts and questions here seem to be really serious and genuine.

Observe – "What do you expect from your spouse?"

– Do you want her or him to be honest and sincere to you or would you accept her or his infidelity and extra-marital affairs?

"What do you expect from your parents and from your children?"

– Would you appreciate if they tell you lies, make you fool, pay no respect, and give no attention, no credibility, no significance to you? Or, would you love to be respected by them, and would like them to be sincere, honest, true to you and have confidence in you?

At your work place, whether it is your office, your shop, some farmland or it is your factory etc. –

"What do you want from your subordinates?"

– Would you appreciate their disobedience, disrespect, a bunch of lies, sugar-coated flowery words and false promises only? Or, would you want them to be sincere, hardworking, upright, honest, obedient and respectful?

The truth is –

"In the world nothing moves without sincerity, honesty, integrity, morals, virtues and other positive attributes."

"The whole system is working everywhere, in order, just because of these attributes only."

Also –

"In the long, run only honesty, sincerity, integrity, morals and virtues win and yield fruits – more so if it is seen in totality, for all-round success in life and for a well-balanced life, having all the five healths.

Be it a job, a business or any other area of life – in the long run the one which is successful and a winner, is the one who rides on these attributes along with that 90 per cent important GS part of education, apart from academics – the TS part of education of 10 per cent importance.

Dangerous Mindsets: Which must be avoided!

Generally, in India particularly, two widespread mindsets of the people hamper their collective and personal growth.

132 ▪ *Wake-Up Call in the Wee Hours*

These both following mindsets are even dangerous like *cancer* to society, from the point of view of community-living and individual happiness both.

Dangerous Mindset 1: Why Me? Why You?

You often come across in life that there is some crime, some mishap, some accident somewhere, or there is any other such situation where people seek help of others – where services of one may be of great help and of great value to others.

But what do you usually hear, see or observe through personal experiences or through media is a growing trend that – "People are not helping people."

The main reason of this rising phenomenon is the attitude of people, the mindset that – "Why me?"

Most of the times, the thinking behind this mindset is – "Not my concern! I will think of only me, mine and I! I am safe or so and so are safe! My.... or I are/ am not in trouble! So, why should I help? What do I lose or gain?" Etc.

And suppose, if you happen to think to volunteer yourself for others, in such a situation, then – "What do you hear? What are you told by your so-called nears and dears and well-wishers?"

Something like – "Why you?"

Thinking pattern behind this mindset to prevent you is – "Why should you bother? Are they your relative or are they your close ones … etc.?"

Usually this mindset of – "Why me? Why you?" – would also be clubbed with various other apprehensions and fears which may be pseudo or which may be real at times. Attached in the packing of the expression of this mindset would be some wrong programming as well.

A Word of Caution-Danger!

But in this mindset, here is a word of caution against a big danger.

Firstly, the obvious danger is – "If you happen to be needing help tomorrow, will you get it?" – Think it! Then in this way, there will be no community-living at all.

Secondly, if you happen to subscribe to this mindset or you had this mindset sometimes back, you need to introspect! Recollect your feelings. You would find that-

"You would never be at ease with yourself." Guilt conscience hits you hard, and hampers your growth.

Dangerous mindset 2: Chalta hai!-It is OK!

That is yet another dangerous mindset – you might have experienced it and observed in your life several times.

If there is any bad event, a bad incident, some unhealthy event, any shoulder-rubbing, any rough-patch or any poor performance, experienced or done either by you or by anyone around you, then this most common phrase only must have been repeated –

"*Chalta hai!* It is OK! Do not bother!"

Here is a subtle point! So long, these words are used with the intention to help reduce one's worries, reduce one's tensions, and help one to avoid any depression or frustration, these may be acceptable because, *"One should never brood over the past!"*

But if these words, this mindset conveys the acceptance or approval of some other alarming things like –

deteriorating standards, lack of performance, lesser quality outputs, reduced exploration of one's potential, or substandard products and services etc.-then it is a big danger to you, to society and to nation even.

This mindset actually is the result of casual attitude and casual-approach.

Casualness is in direct contrast to sincerity.

And, without sincerity, nothing can be achieved in life.

Just imagine for a moment, the few scenarios as shown in adjacent pictures – to be happening in your life!

Ask yourself now –

"Would you like it all?"

And if you were at the receiving end, then –

"How and what would you feel? What would you expect from others?"

Think! – If you do not like it now, then

– "Why you don't like it now? Why it is not acceptable to you now?"

– "This 'chalta hai' mindset is detrimental to striving for excellence! It

is against the principle of betterment and improvement. It hampers individual growth."

– "This is the mindset that prevents your best performance, talent and your full potential from coming out, from being tapped and from being explored fully!"

– "This is the mindset, which prevents you from realising your 'dreams'."

And when as individual, you do not deliver your best, you do not perform at your 'best level', the society suffers and in turn the whole nation suffers!

You must avoid these dangerous mindsets.

Part–IV

The Way Out!
"Where there is a will, there is a way!"

Part-IV

The Way Out

"If there is a will, there is a way."

14

Wake-Up Calls

"Wake up!" The first call!

The first call, in these wee-hours, is a wake-up call!

The first step towards way-out in these times of chaos, despair and hopelessness, is to wake-up.

That is what you hear in this silence amidst chaos:

..."WAKE-UP!"...

First step starts with you!

Life takes its toll upon you first! First victim of these difficult times, challenges, chaotic situations, circumstances and of various other factors is-you!

Your dreams, desires and aspirations, your talents and potential, your beliefs and convictions, your good habits and attitudes, your identity, individuality and originality, your overall growth, your values, self-esteem, and ultimately your happiness, joy of life, balance and stability – these are the first casualties.

Some of these have either taken place already or some are going to take place shortly, in this present smoky and polluted environment around, in these wee hours.

That calls for the first step, the first effort, and the first prevention too.

And, "that first step is-you!"
All of it has to start, in the world around you, with you!
And, you only can combat it!
Definitely you will not find yourself alone in taking this *first step*-now onwards!

Is your dream intact?

You snatch a toy from a child and observe its reaction. You might have to face a feeling of loss, some cry, hauling, stiff resistance or even violent struggle.

This is the reaction of a child, who physically, mentally, and emotionally has still a long way to go and grow up. And this reaction is for a toy, a mere toy, may be even worth a few tens of paisas only – may be some waste thing like an empty toothpaste-tube, or an empty powder-can etc. But, for the child at that moment it is the most precious thing in the world, which he may never want to give up so easily, without resistance or without some expression of protest.

Well – "What about you?" – you are not a child. You are a grown-up, well-built, educated, rugged, well-experienced, and a capable-competent man or woman. And the thing dearest to you is not a mere toy-rather it is a thing which is well-cherished for long, is nurtured well with care and is within your reach – it is 'your dream'.

Has somebody already snatched your dream from you? Or have you allowed your dream to be stolen by somebody from you?

– Or your dream is still intact like a precious and priceless possession treasured with you still.

You are the victim, the judge here.

Just check it! Your miseries, frustrations, disgust, anger, displeasure, discomfort, unhappiness and a feeling of defeat, of loss-all of it – is it as well as not because somebody has either stolen your dreams or has just crushed those mercilessly? Or, because you yourself have given-up your dreams, allowing your talent and your potential to decay down the drain, or even let it be misused at times. Or, because you have given up all hopes of realising it all, facing various challenges and difficulties in it. Check it out. You do need to take a stock of situation.

How would you feel when your dream comes true?

Scene 1
Just imagine, if you wish to have some delicious food one day. And, your spouse or your beloved arranges for it. Or, someone offers you a treat of the same menu, you wished for.

"How would you feel then?"

Scene 2
Imagine, if you desire or dream of some particular wear-some suit, shirt, trousers, shoes, wrist-watch, hat, goggles or tie etc., or some sari, salwar-suit, skirt, night gown, bellies, sandals, ornaments or cap etc.

And your spouse, fiancée or somebody else *gifts* it to you. "How would you feel then?"

Scene 3

Or imagine, if you wish to *visit* a certain place, or travel a particular tourist-spot.

And some of your rich relative, a friend or your company sponsors it for you, may be with your family.

"How would you feel then?"

Obviously you would feel elated. Well, when such considerably smaller issues, possessions or events can give abundant joy and pleasure to you, just think – "How much more joy, happiness, satisfaction, fulfilment, gratification and self-worth you will feel, when you would be able to nurture your talent and put it to some worthy, noble, satisfying cause?"

"How would you feel when you would be able to make all your dreams come true?"

So – "wake up!"

And just think of your dream!"

Think of that moment in your life when your dream would come true and decide, where you wanted to reach or where you still want to reach?"

Your destinations: Check where are you going to land?

You wanted to be happy and satisfied. You planned your life to be comfortable. You did foresee luxuries and comforts for you and for your dearest ones around, in your lifetime itself.

You wanted to get the best, to have the best and to give your best to the people around you in your life – best in terms of money, comforts, possessions, performance, services, and your contributions in various forms. You dreamt of being a giver and a provider in life etc.

Certainly, you did not foresee or dream yourself ever to be a drunkard, a drug addict, a convict behind bars etc. Also, you surely did not plan to be a person dejected, disappointed, frustrated, mentally-physically sick, financially broke or under debts etc.

May be you are thinking that – you did never dream to be on top of the world or to be on worst note of life either.

But then – "did you really plan to be just a mediocre, all through your life? And as a mediocre person also, are you going to be happy, satisfied, comfortable?"

"If you do not change direction in life, then you will continue to move in the same old direction, and therefore you will reach to the destination where you never wanted to be. You will get, which you never planned for."

That is why it is high time now when – "you must check direction of your life, and you must know your dreams."

You definitely need to know –

"Is this the destination where you are heading to, that you always dreamt of?"

"Is this the thing you are going to get, which you always longed for?"

"Is this what you are going to be, what you always wanted to be?"

Sure enough, once knowing your dreams and aspirations, you need to take stock of the situation and check –

"Where are you going to land if you do not change direction of your life's aeroplane now?"

15

Are You Worried – Find Your Dream and Be a Player

Why should you be concerned?

Case 1: It doesn't affect me!
Consider few following news you read or someone told you:–

"So and so politician made so much money by looting government department or by looting us. So and so bureaucrat is corrupt and is not doing his job, which causes trouble to society."

"India lost cricket match to Australia. Your soccer or hockey team is out of tournament. Your Olympic squad returned empty-handed this time too."

"Your state is rated the most backward and poor. There was a dacoity last night in your township. Somebody snatched a gold chain from a lady in your street."

"So and so you know, went bankrupt. Oh! Mrs Sharma's daughter eloped with Mr Rao's son. Your friend's son failed in school exams. Your so and so relative had a family feud last week! And so on...!"

Just ask yourself –

"Does it all bother you? Are you worried?"

In all probability, your answer would be-no.

Even if you say yes, then ask yourself –

"Oh! Really! Are you really worried?"

And your response would be now – "Well, no... Yah, I am... But not much... You see...!"

The point is that in all such above cases and likely scenarios *you* might have conditioned your mind already. You might say –

"*Chalta hai* – It's OK! It does not affect me *directly*." Etc.

Yes, you can comfortably choose to ignore all such happenings, occurrences, and events, just by palming-off yourself with words like –

"*Chalta hai* – It's O.K. Why should I bother? Why should I be concerned? I am not affected. My family is not affected. What can I do about it? Not my responsibility. Somebody else is responsible for it. So and so...is to be blamed for it. So and so...only should retrieve the situation now" etc.

That is true.

You are hundred per cent correct.

Case 2: Enough! Why all this to me only?

Consider now another few scenarios:-

You go to some government office and find, your job cannot be done until you grease the palms of concerned peon, clerk, bureaucrat or a politician.

You were practicing for a match, for months, and your team loses the match, in spite of your best performance.

Your son took part in all sports and debate competitions at school, and returned empty-handed, this time too – no medals, no prizes.

Your family is considered as illiterate, poor, or backward.

You had gone for a movie show with your family and when you returned, you found that, somebody had cleaned your house in the meantime – all your valuables and treasures were stolen.

Your father is on the verge of bankruptcy! Yesterday somebody snatched a gold chain from your mother's neck. Your daughter or sister eloped with a street-rowdy boy. Your son failed in 12th exams. You are heading for divorce with your spouse. And so on...!

"What would you say now?"

Something like – "Oh, God! Enough now. Please shut-up now. No more can I listen or read such things and visualise these. Why all this is to happen to me only?"

Surely, all this must be evoking disgust, anger, frustration or even a feeling of vengeance in you, towards authors – for daring to tell you and make you imagine such rubbish, such unimaginable things. True, and we are sorry for that.

But Mr.... or Ms... so and so (read your name here) just think for a moment –

"Why does it all bother you now? Why do you feel all such emotions now, in this case-2 ?"

Can you still afford to say with the same cool and ease as in case-1 you said that "Chalta hai! It's ok. It does not affect me?"

"Why are you concerned now? Why do you bother now? Are you really worried now?"

Just think – "if...! Yes if, it happens to you or to your...so and so then whose responsibility it is? Are you not to be blamed at all – not even partially? Who can and who will best solve your these riddles?"

Friend, all this bothers you now, because now you are closely affected. Or someone close to you is affected, is troubled, or has failed – that is why you too are concerned now. That is the reason. That is why you are worried now.

"Is it not the truth?" Check it out!

Probably, you will find that – "Yes! That is the reason."

Case 3: Feeling of loss!
Consider these few scenes now:

You had been gifted by your spouse or by your beloved, a beautiful leather purse, with your name embossed on it. Just while entering a movie theatre, somebody pick-pocketed it.

You had a gold-plated pen, which was much dearer to you, for some personal fond memories. You never went anywhere without it. And, last time when you went on a tour for your work, you forgot to pick it back from the hotel room and lost it.

You had a dry flower – a rose, kept very carefully in your childhood-diary. This flower always reminded you of a friend, whom you missed in the journey of life. And one day you find, rats or moth has eaten it away, with the diary too.

Surely you might be having some dress, some cloth, which you may never be going to wear, but you treat it as a treasure. And, that dress gets burnt in a house-fire.

You feel a loss in all such cases-some irreparable loss, a void.

Whenever you will recall your memories related to these, taking you back in the past, and you happen to recollect these instances, you would experience pain.

Think –

"Why?"

Because, you have some emotions, some memories, or some dreams attached to those things.

You are concerned because your dream is like your baby,

Whenever, someone even poses any threat to your long-cherished dreams or to your highly personal, emotionally attached possessions or treasures, you are surely concerned!

You are worried, bothered because –

"Like breath is to your body, sweet emotions and memories are to your mind, your dreams are to your life!" You just cannot afford to part away with it. Can you?

And if there is some threat, any kind of threat – remotest or even if very mild threat to your treasured possessions, to those long cherished dreams of yours – you would go all out to protect those.

Now you want to safeguard those. That is why you are worried. That is why you need to bother.

"Can you allow someone to steal those worthy possessions – dreams from you, from your life?"

"Can you allow someone to smash your dreams and walk over them?"

"Never! Never you would allow it!"

That is your reason to be touchy about it.

That exactly is the reason, which propels you further to action.

That is the reason you protect your dreams and nurture them, just like a cute little baby, an infant, cuddling in your arms, close to your heart.

Your reasons: *Your dream!*

Reasons only make one to work, to act, and to put-in efforts.

Reasons result in actions!

Journey by a train

Imagine you are travelling in a train. Train is running at fast speed. Someone asks you, "Jump out from the train."

Chances are you will not.

You will think – 'From moving train! Speed is high I may get hurt. Terrain is also bad. And, why should I jump out? Is this man asking me to jump out crazy or what?" And you do not jump out from the train.

150 ■ Wake-Up Call in the Wee Hours

Shortly after this, you hear some noises like, "Fire! Fire! Train has caught fire!" And, someone shouts in mid-air, "Jump out!"

And you...! Sure enough, you would not even think. You would straightaway head for the door, and jump out from the train, running fast at whatever speed it is.

"What caused such response?"

... Reason! Now, you had a reason.

So, find out – "What is your reason? What is your dream? Do you have a dream?"

Check it out!

That would be the reason you may be concerned for, worried or bothered for.

"Why do not you make it happen, make it true, make your reason a reality!"

"How long would you allow yourself to be kicked around?"

A player and a football

"Have you ever played football? Or you must have seen a Soccer match. What do you see on the football ground?"

On a football ground there are only two major entities. Either a football player, which could be of any team, of your side or of opposition-or the second entity is football itself.

Are You Worried – Find Your Dream and Be ...

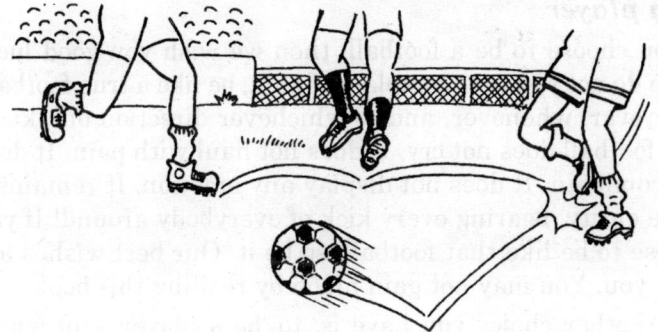

A football is the entity, which gets kicked around – all over the ground. A player kicks it from this corner it goes to other side. Another player kicks it from that direction it goes to yet another player, to get another kick...! And the game continues.

Players are those who give direction, a kick, some push to a football, and control all its movements.

So is the life! In the life too, there are several football matches being played daily, with you and around you. There is no escape.

You have only one choice to make, out of two.

> 1. **Be a Player! Or**
> 2. **Be a Football!**

Decide – "What do you want to be?"

A player or a football.

For argument sake, one can cite, two more entities in a football ground-that is time and a referee!

Well, here in life too, time is a crucial factor, and referee here is the outcome – means whatever happens to you!

Here is only one difference-between a football ground and your life: –

"You have the choice here, in life. You can choose to be a player or a football."

Be a player

If you choose to be a football, then we wish you good luck. Then do not you ever complain of pain, be like a true football. Wherever, whenever, and to whichever direction one kicks it, a football does not cry. It does not haul with pain. It does not complain. It does not display any emotion. It remains a mute entity, bearing every kick of everybody around! If you choose to be like that football, so be it. Our best wishes are with you. You may not gain much by reading this book.

Another choice you have is, to 'be a player' – of which team – can be an after-thought and it can be dealt later. But first, if you decide to be a football-player, although it is good, but remember, you have to know three things first.

To be a player

You need to know:
1. **Rules of the game**
2. *What to develop and what to equip yourself with?*
3. *How to be a good player?*

Then:
- *Be a good player!*
- *Practice, action!!*

Firstly, you will have to learn the 'rules of the game." Every game has its own set of rules. Here too, it is so.

Are You Worried – Find Your Dream and Be ... ■ 153

Secondly, you need to know – 'What you need to develop in yourself and what you need to equip yourself with?' Like- you need to *develop* your stamina, strength, endurance, posture, and knowledge of game-you need to equip yourself with proper kit, shoes, special wears, art of doing it, apart from attitude, beliefs and skills.

Thirdly, you must know – 'How to become a good player? – What does it involve? What are the attributes and qualities of a good and a successful player? And, how to develop those in you?'

After knowing all these three important things, what you need to do is, just two things –

> *Practice! Practice!! Practice!!!*

> **ACTION**

Be in motion always! Never remain static!

That is the reason you got to be concerned of yourself. You got to take parameters of life, under your control. -Else others in the world would keep making you dance like a puppet.

Decide again – "Does it all bother you?"

"Are you worried?"

Here the words worry and botheration, symbolise your awakening and concern for you.

> *If you are worried –*
> *Wake-up first, find your dream,*
> *and be a player!*

16

Think and Analyse

"Everything in the world has a cause and effect relationship!"

An overall perspective

"Life goes on like a trance-a state of deep-sleep!"

Most of the time you become so engrossed in your current activities, jobs, problems, and petty gains that you lose the overall perspective.

Just look at any picture around – may be some scenery or a painting.

Look at it very closely.... more closely... more closely... some further close.

Go so close to it that distance between your nose and the picture you are looking at, remains less than three inches.

"What do you see now? Can you see the painting? Can you see the scenery?"

No! Instead of it, you see a blurred image only.

So is the life!

"Every now and then you have to step back a little and see the overall perspective of things, of events and of all experiences in life."

Then only you understand the process and see the clear picture.

The whole design then becomes clear to you."

An exercise

After understanding the processes involved and what has gone wrong with you in life – you need to take a step back!

Take some time. Introspect! Look at your life so far. Take a while to think deeply, and analyse by yourself, the following few things.

The only caution is that – "You must think yourself! – You shouldn't be borrowing others' thinking or others' opinions – that you have done enough, in life so far!" The answers of these following issues should be your own, and then only you would be benefitted most.

Also, you must analyse it by yourself only. Do not consult it with others. Do not hang out on others, like some cribbing, complaining, crying babies! Be your own person, the person inside you, while doing this exercise. Exert your own mind a little. "How long you will continue to keep it in safe custody – in a trunk under lock?"

"Your mind increases by expenditure! The more you use it, the more it is sharpened."

"The more you distribute your knowledge, the more it increases."

You need to answer these to yourself only.

*Ask yourself
the following three questions!*

A.	*Were you wrong in school or college?* *Is dreaming wrong?*
B.	*Should transitions not be there?*
C.	*Can you change your present?*

Think! Analyse! Introspect!

Let your natural thoughts and your natural response to these questions come out. You may like to write down these answers coming to your mind right now.

Don't try to palm-off – by skipping it or shirking yourself – or by simply fooling you with answers like – "I do not know!" Do not do that stunt now. You might have done it enough, throughout your life so far. You must be having your own answers to these questions. Let those be spelt out by you, to yourself only.

Pause here!

Take your time and complete this exercise first, before reading further. It is very important for you to know your own dreams, your beliefs, and your attitudes.

Use this answer space to note your answers now:-

> **Answers:**
> **A.**
> **B.**
> **C.**

All right, if you have finished this exercise, you may read further now to consider the following answers and views.

Question-A: *"Were you wrong in school or college? — Is dreaming wrong?"*

> **The** *answer* **is:** *no! not at all!*

Whatever you must have learnt and whatever process you might have undergone at school or college, you did develop some dreams and some aspirations.

From the time when you were an infant, till you became a grown-up man or woman – some of your dreams became stronger, while some of your aspirations also grew up.

But that is good! Absolutely no fault!

If somebody says that you learnt something wrong at school or at college – it is not true. That is not the case.

The only thing is – "during your those formative years at school or college you were not told the ways and means that how to turn your dreams into reality?

Also, instead of supportive, creative and healthy environment, which would have been helpful to nurture and fulfil your aspirations and dreams, the environment there actually discouraged you and disappointed you.

"The negative influences and imprints were more strongly pumped in you, instead of giving you some more healthy and positive strokes."

But as far as individually you are concerned, you had absolutely no fault. You were right in your thinking, dreaming and aspiring.

All creations are results of somebody's some dream sometime. If you look around and go through history also, you will find that all inventions, discoveries, and creations of excellence, have been existent first as somebody's dream only. Then only these were turned into reality.

Day-dreaming is termed bad. It means if one has dreams and does not work for it at all, that is bad. It would not fetch any growth or happiness.

There is a saying – *"Do not make your horses of your imaginations and of your dreams, run high in the air."*

But what is commonly missed, is a corollary to it:

"If you run horses of your dreams high in the air first, then only one day you can make them land, make them run on ground too and turn your those dreams into reality-else not."

Question-B: "Should transitions not be there?"

> **The answer is:**
> **No! transitions are natural!**

Transitions from past to present, and from present to future are just natural. You were an infant, grew as a child to an adolescent, then to an adult and would also grow old. It is all a natural process. These transitions have to take place, in everyone's life.

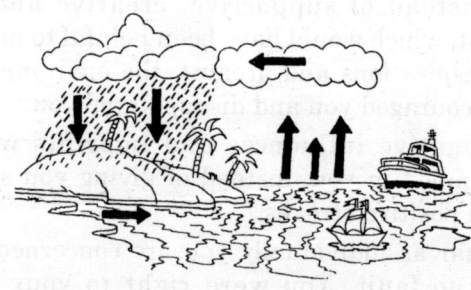

Along with each stage in life, and level of your mental growth at that stage, you do experience transitions in your dreams, your thinking, and in your behaviour too.

But here is a difference – "The long-cherished dreams of yours do not have much transitions." These do not necessarily change with time, whereas your beliefs and your convictions may change at every stage of your growth!

So long, all these transitions lead you to grow in the direction where your aspirations are met, your dreams become a reality, or where at least you are sure of moving in direction of success – it is good. It is healthy for you.

Otherwise also transitions will still be there. But the only thing in your hand is – "instead of these transitions defocusing you, you can choose to control that environment."

Nothing in the world is ever stationary. Everything is moving. The moon revolves around the earth, the earth around the sun, and sun also is moving in the galaxy.

"Is there anything in the universe, which does not undergo transitions?"

Think and Analyse ▪ 159

Yes, there is one and the only thing – "laws of nature!" These have always been the same – were earlier, are today, and what these will be in future!

Examples of laws of nature are like Law of Gravitation – an apple falls on earth, instead of going up in sky, or law of life and death – Everything that has taken birth is to die. Everything else in the universe other than laws of nature undergoes transitions.

But here is a question for you –

"Transitions will always be there. You may choose positive growth or you may choose negative growth. Which one would you like to choose for yourself?"

That is your choice! And that is what, which will govern your future too. You can choose to steer all transitions in life, in nature around, in you, in your thinking, attitudes, beliefs, and in your convictions etc. All to your favour! You can steer all these towards your success in life.

Question-C: "Can you change your present?"

Yes! That is a million-dollar question! That is the question, answer to which may be having most effective, influential, efficient, long-lasting and fast result-bearing consequences for you.

"Can you change your surroundings? Can you change your circumstances? Can you change your environment? Can you change, guide and influence all factors governing your present?"

The answer is:

yes! and no!

There are two things, which influence, govern and control your present!

Internal factors and External factors

Internal factors are more effective and more important. These are like – your beliefs, convictions, thinking and attitudes, your approach to things and to life as a whole, your dreams and your commitment to your dreams, how serious and committed you are to your dreams, your earnestness to change yourself and your adaptability. Your level of competence, skills, knowledge, effort-level and your actions are other important internal factors.

External factors are like – your parents, your place of birth, your society and the community, city, state, and country you belong to; your school, college and teachers there, your economic background, your financial health; your physical limitations or any handicaps you have, your family, personal, social responsibilities and liabilities; the state of industrial-agricultural development of your area, various policies of government, various socio-economic, geological, political or geographical factors; crime-rate, law and order situation, nature's gifts or calamities etc. All of those factors, which are not directly under your control are external factors.

Crux of the matter is – "If you try to change the external factors, which are not directly under your control, you may be able to change those or you may not! But if you try to change the internal factors, surely"

Here is the elaboration of answer to this 'Question C' – "Can you change your present?" –

No – certainly if you try to change your present – without even understanding the process involved by merely trying to change others, or by trying to change **the external factors** only. No you cannot change your present this way.

Yes – If you change yourself first, change your internal factors, and subsequently control those. Certainly can! You can definitely then change your present.

Change your goggles!

Suppose you go to a beautiful mountain, with your friends and dear ones, on a holiday trip. There are all the beauties of nature around-beautiful pink-rose flowers, deep-blue clear water, lush greenery around, and mountain giving you feelings of pleasure and uplifting thoughts! A beautiful sight! But you are wearing a dark-grey coloured goggles.

"What do you see then? Can you see all the greenery, blue water, blue sky, and pink-roses etc. in their natural colours?" – no!

You may carry on an endless debate with your friends and those dear ones, regarding *true colours* of those gifts of nature. Will that debate still make you see the nature's beauty, in its natural colours, and feel pleasure?

"Is there a way to change this present of yours, your surroundings, so that you can appreciate and enjoy nature's gifts scattered around there!"

Yes! There is a way!

It is very simple! A kid around there, just points towards your glasses – the goggles you are sporting. The moment you remove it the whole sight is changed. You can really appreciate, love and enjoy the nature now. Your present is changed.

Only difference in life is that, here the goggle is inside your mind. "All your internal factors are your goggles."

So long, you continue to put-on goggles of dark-grey colour, your attitude, beliefs, convictions, thinking and your actions too, all are tainted dark. They are all negative and degenerating. You do not see the beauties around.

But the moment you change the colour of your goggles and you put-on plain transparent glasses – you correct, realign and cleanse your thoughts, beliefs, convictions and commitments, and you take proper actions in right directions. Your present does change certainly.

Your life and world around you would change, because now your goggles, your perceptions are changed.

17

Solution Steps: What Should You Do? What Can You Do? How Can You Succeed?

"Every problem in the world has its solution too!"
"Think! Learn-Why, What and How! Act on it! Succeed!"

> • *It's your life!*
> • *You are the captain of your ship!*
> • *Sink it or sail it through!*
> • *You are responsible for it!*
>
> *What can you change?*

Solving a problem

1. The very first step towards solving any problem is to realise and acknowledge, that there is some problem. Accept that something exists which needs change and correction.
2. Then the second step is to find reason – why the problem needs a solution? Why change is needed?

3. The third step would be the solution – how you can do it?

Same is in your life!

Your life!

1. The very first thing in life is to realise that – "You can change your life!"
2. Secondly, you should know that – "why should you change your life?" In the nutshell you must be sure that – "by this change you can achieve whatever you want" – you can realise your goals, whatever you set your eyes upon!
3. Thirdly, understand that, this how part is a bit subtle. You do not need to change things externally, rather you need to change things internally first.

Recollect that if you catch some infection in your body, or some plant develops some disease, then – "How do you treat it? Do you treat symptoms or do you treat disease?"

Also decide – "what gives long-term relief?"

Probably you would say – "by medicines, to cure internally, and then treat externally. Or may be, simultaneously treat both!"

You can change your life!

Yes! YOU CAN CHANGE YOUR LIFE.
You can change your life by changing:
1. YOURSELF *first!*
2. *Your PRESENT – your circumstances.*
3. *Influence your DESTINY – your future.*

- Yes! Have this faith in you.
- *Believe* it! Believe yourself!
- *Believe in your dreams! Believe in your potential.*
- You can *control* things.
- *You can change – yourself,* your *present,* and your *future!*

Process involved – What is needed?

The **process of change** – of *you, your life, your present and your future*-does involve four major things, four factors. These are the essential ingredients towards achieving whatever you want in life and towards success in life.

> *Four factors involved in the process*
> 1. *your environment*
> 2. *conditioning of your mind*
> 3. *your thinking, attitudes and beliefs*
> 4. *your effort-level*

1. Your environment

Assume you reap a plant in a *flower pot* and a *similar plant* you reap in an open area *in soil* – where it gets proper air, sun, natural water and unlimited scope for growth.

Think it now –

"Where would that plant grow better?"

"Which plant would gain more height?"

"What's the difference?"

The key word in your answer would be –
"Environment!"

Environment is that, which makes the whole difference here!

2. Conditioning of your mind

"Correct *environment conditions your mind* in a correct way."

You are required to put *directed and sustained efforts to condition* the conscious and subconscious parts of your mind, in a correct way.

Conditioning of your mind is that, what makes the whole difference between successful and unsuccessful, between achievers and non-achievers.

"Whom do you listen to?"
– That also conditions your mind!

3. Your thinking, attitudes and beliefs

"Every creation by a human being is always created first in the mind."

That depends upon – "How do you think?" It also depends upon – "What are your attitudes?" – Towards yourself, towards your goals and dreams, towards your potential, capabilities, skills and knowledge, and towards others.

Further it also depends upon-"What do you talk to yourself? What do you believe-in?"

> *Environment and thus conditioning of your mind governs-your thinking, your attitudes and your beliefs!*

Answers to these above questions and related things only, will decide for you –

"What you are and what you can be?"

"What you do and what you can do?"

"What you have and what you can have?"

4. Your effort-level

Right environment conditions your mind in the right way, and you develop correct thinking, attitudes and beliefs.

But still, all this can be a waste if you lack in action-in effort-level.

Ultimately, the deciding factor is –

"How much efforts-level you put-in? Do you put-in any efforts at all or you merely think and dream?"

If you are not putting in any efforts towards your dreams, then it would be called day-dreaming only, and you would surely be a laughing stock!

An action, an effort and a decision to try your best are the words you require for your **success** and for **achievement** in the end.

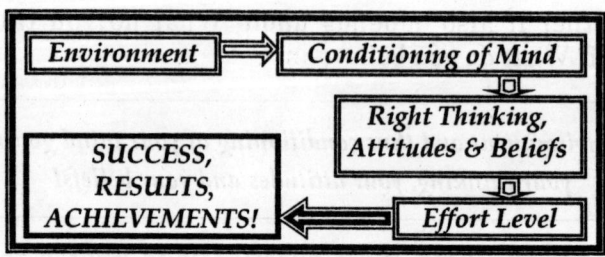

Steps to way-out: A journey to success!

To *achieve* what you *want* in life, to *realise* what you *dream* of, to *explore* your full *potential,* to *actualise* the *creative abilities of your heart and mind,* and to *be in* the best *environment and outlet*, following are the suggested steps.

These steps have been observed, experienced and laid down by all *successful people*, all *dreamers* and *achievers* and by all *performers* of the whole world, in all times.

These are the steps, which have also been told by all *saints, prophets, priests* and all *champions of all the worthy causes and pursuits,* in India and across the globe.

Combined with life-experiences and analysis by our team, here are the steps *which can change your life too!*

Step 1: "Help yourself!"
"Self-help is the best help!"

Therefore you can do the following:

1. Explore yourself.

Wake-Up! Decide that —
- What you want to be, want to do and want to have?
- Where you wanted to reach? Where are you going? And, where will you land?
- What are your potentials and your capabilities? Check your assets.

2. Positive feeding to brain
- Feed positive, good, mental-food, to your brain regularly to stay healthy.

3. Associate to positives
- Associate yourself with positive and right people.
- Have positive thinking and attitudes.
- Take only positive inputs.
- Be in positive environment.

> **Step 1:** *Help yourself!*
> 1. *Explore yourself*
> 2. *Positive feeding to mind*
> 3. *Associate to positives*
> 4. *Explore four sources of help*

4. Explore four sources of help.
- *Books* – Books are all-time great friends, and a great source of learning.
- *Audio-Cassettes and CDs* – Right music and lectures of successful and right kind of people do help you greatly.
- *Nature* – It has been said that – "Nature is a great teacher!" – and it is the best teacher. Just observe it and learn.
- *People* – Company of uplifted, wise and evolved people does really shape you. Their lectures, teachings and seminars etc. do help you in many, better and effective ways.

Step 2: "Learn!"
You need to *learn* and *acquire* three important things:
1. Skill
- Know first – What, Why and How?
- Know the difference of 10 per cent and 90 per cent education.

- Learn and acquire right skills. You should be sure first, why you need it? Use effective and efficient methods for it.

2. Knowledge
   - Know what you need to know?
   - Find, why you need to know it?
   - And be sure, how can you get this knowledge faster and in an efficient way?
   - Get that 90 per cent important knowledge.

> **Step 2:** *Learn*
> 1. *Skills*
> 2. *Knowledge*
> 3. *Focus*

3. Focus
   - Learn to focus.
   - Learn to focus at right things.
   - Focus things in the right perspective, with correct-angle and approach, and at the right time.

Step 3: "Develop habits! have self-discipline!"
You then need to develop right discipline, self-discipline.

There should be **no external judge** – no external rewards, punishments or fear-motivation.

"Eradicate all carrots and sticks from your life!"

You need to develop the following right habits and things for this:

- *Reading books, listening to right lectures and music, attending right lectures and seminars.*
- *Company and environment influences you and affects your life significantly. Therefore you must keep yourself in good company and right environment, which should be healthy and conducive for internal growth.*

- *Will-power and persistence are key to success in life. Have positive feelings towards your goals, dreams and your objectives. Strengthen your determination, will power and convictions! Have persistence! Never say quit or die. Never ever give-up.*

> **Step 3:** *Develop habits and discipline for*
> 1. *Reading and listening*
> 2. *Company and environment*
> 3. *Will-Power and persistence*

And to summarise

> Find your *Dream!*
> Be a *Player!*
> Change your *Internal Factors!*

> Choose your *Goal* in Life!
> *Achieve* it!
> YOU CAN DO IT!

> Be in
> **Correct Environment**
> around YOU!
>
> *Create* it!
> *Build* it! And,
> *Help creating* it!